How to be an Advanced Driver

How to be an Advanced Driver

PUBLISHED IN ASSOCIATION WITH THE
INSTITUTE OF ADVANCED MOTORISTS

Published 2004 by
Motorbooks International
23 Montpelier Vale
Blackheath
London SE3 OTJ

Cover photo reprinted with permission from Jaguar UK.

Edited by Mark Hughes
Photography by James Mann
Designed by Bruce Aiken
Typeset by Sarah Ward

ISBN 0-7603-2037-3
Printed in Great Britain
by Butler & Tanner
Frome, Somerset

ACKNOWLEDGEMENTS
Grateful thanks are due to the following for their assistance in illustrating this book: Claire Doughty, Caroline Everard, Edward Herridge, Tim Hughes, Anthony Lanaway, Martin Williams, Transport Research Laboratory (Frank Pond), Rover Group Ltd (Glenys Fairchild), Vauxhall Motors Ltd (Jackie Green), BMW (GB) Ltd (Alun Parry), Metropolitan Police Photo Library, The Shout Picture Company (John Callan), The Volvo Magazine (Patrick Devereux), Swift Caravans (Charlotte Le Blond) and The Automobile Association.

How to use this book

This book is designed to be used both for self-study and to supplement expert tuition. The way it is organised in themes and topics allows you quickly to find the information you need, so that you can refer to it regularly as you develop individual areas of your driving technique. The most important topics are conveniently summarised at the end of each chapter under the headings 'Advanced checklist' and 'What the examiner looks for'. When you have absorbed and practised all the skills, you should be able to pass the Advanced Driving Test with ease. Improving your technique, however, is a never-ending process, so remember to use this book to brush up on your skills throughout your driving career.

Contents

ADVANCED
INSTITUTE
MOTORISTS
IAM

1 PRINCIPLES OF ADVANCED DRIVING

The need for advanced driving

The toll on the roads

Deaths and injuries on Britain's roads have been falling steadily since the war, even though today there are more vehicles on our roads than ever before.

Many factors have contributed to this trend. Hundreds of towns have been bypassed, new roads are engineered to very high standards, and some of the most dangerous junctions have been improved. Even though you may not think it, our motorway network has never been better. Modern cars offer more protection in accidents, and enormous improvements in handling, roadholding, braking and steering help drivers to avoid accidents. Speeding in dangerous places is being confronted by new technology, while drink driving, at last, is generally regarded as socially unacceptable.

Yet the number of people who die on our roads remains unacceptably high – the toll is still over 3000 a year. Traffic accidents are the largest cause of death and injury among young adults, ahead of illness and drug abuse. Nearly a quarter of all adults who die before they are 30 lose their lives in road accidents. Regardless of age, almost half of all accidental deaths in Britain occur on the roads.

Despite the progress that has been made, one area still has to be tackled – driving standards. This is where you can play your part. If every driver in Britain developed his or her skills to the standard required to pass the Advanced Driving Test, deaths and injuries would fall spectacularly.

You have shown an interest in improving your driving abilities by picking up this book with a view to taking the Advanced Driving Test. Encourage your friends and family to do the same. So much pain and suffering would be avoided if Britain could become a nation of advanced drivers.

The automatic camera is just one of the numerous factors behind the welcome decrease in deaths and injuries on British roads. But one area – driving standards – still leaves plenty of room for improvement.

Advanced driving is safer driving

Mechanical or tyre failures account for a tiny proportion of accidents. Most accidents – around 95 per cent – are caused by human error. Road safety ultimately depends on the skill and responsibility of everyone who drives. The motto of the Institute of Advanced Motorists (IAM), which was formed in 1956 to work for higher standards of driving, is 'skill with responsibility'.

Advanced driving, as you will see, is based on a set of fundamental principles which guide every action you ever take behind the wheel of a car. As an advanced driver, you control your car with precision, you drive with intense concentration and awareness, you anticipate danger and mistakes from other drivers, and you always leave a comfortable margin for safety.

Drivers who have passed the Advanced Driving Test have a 50-70 per cent lower accident rate than the average driver.

This does not mean that you drive at a snail's pace, forever anxious about the next danger to appear in your path. Advanced drivers are confident and decisive, but never reckless. They are enthusiastic about driving and make better progress than most drivers, choosing carefully the moments when they overtake and searching for chances to move unobtrusively through traffic. They tend to be ahead of the game without anyone else noticing.

If you play a sport, you constantly aim to improve your performance and play more competitively without breaking the rules. If you are ambitious at work, you pour immense energy into fulfilling challenges and achieving promotion.

Why not put the same quest for high standards into your driving? Advanced driving is all about achieving, for your own and everyone's good. It can bring enormous satisfaction, as well as having such a significant effect on safety that some insurers offer substantial discounts if you pass the Advanced Driving Test.

Statistics compiled by the Transport Research Laboratory show that IAM members – all of whom have passed the Advanced Driving Test – have a 25 per cent lower accident rate than candidates who fail, and a 50-70 per cent better record than the average driver. IAM members not only have fewer accidents, but those in which they are involved tend to be less serious.

Advanced drivers are confident and decisive, but never reckless. They are enthusiastic about driving and make better progress than most drivers.

After you pass the L-test

Apart from the addition of a simple multiple-choice written assessment, the government driving test has remained unchanged since 1934. You can pass it largely without demonstrating more than the most basic grasp of driving skills, and without ever driving on a motorway or at night.

Passing the L-test marks the end of an apprenticeship and the start of the real learning that develops as you put miles under your belt. If you are interested in demonstrating a higher level of skill behind the wheel, you should aim to pass the Advanced Driving Test.

How your driving can deteriorate

Almost all of us have a high opinion of our driving, yet the perfect driver has yet to be created. After passing the L-test, many drivers develop bad habits – excessively late braking, a cavalier attitude in traffic or over-ambitious overtaking – which show they still have much to learn.

With thought and study, the high standards of skill explained in this book should make you assess your driving with fresh eyes. Passing your L-test is just the beginning of your driving career. By putting the advice in this book into practice, you will be able to improve your driving every time you make a journey.

Comfort and safety

Driving position

The correct driving position: arms and legs are in a comfortable position, and the steering wheel is held at 'ten-to-two' or 'quarter-to-three'.

The correct driving position makes you feel comfortable, alert and in control. You should hold the wheel in either the 'ten-to-two' or 'quarter-to-three' position. Your arms should be slightly bent at the elbows at an angle of between 90 and 120 degrees. Your legs should be bent at the knees when your feet touch the pedals.

The stretched arms and legs position of a racing driver is of no use in an ordinary road car. It prevents you using the steering wheel properly and increases fatigue, and may also reduce your field of vision if it causes you to sit lower.

Timid drivers often sit too close to the wheel, a posture which increases tension and restricts control of the steering. This position suggests that a driver lacks confidence in handling a car, although poor eyesight is another reason. A driver may be unaware of any defect in vision – deterioration generally creeps up gradually – but compensates for it unconsciously by sitting as close as possible to the windscreen.

If you share the use of a car with other people, the chances are that you will have to make at least three adjustments before turning the ignition key. The seat may have to be moved forwards or backwards, the angle of the seat backrest may have to be altered, and mirrors may have to be adjusted.

You can make the mistake of being too relaxed. It may feel comfortable to hold the steering wheel low down only with the right hand, with elbow resting on the door pull or window sill, but control in an emergency is severely impaired. One-handed steering – perhaps with the hand casually holding a spoke of the wheel – suggests over-confidence, almost to the point of boredom.

The driver of a car with power steering needs to be especially aware of developing lazy habits.

Too far back: stretched arms and legs reduce control and increase fatigue.

Too close: this position increases tension, restricts steering control and requires the hands to hold the wheel in the wrong place.

Mirrors

Mirrors should be kept clean and properly adjusted. People brushing past your car while it is parked sometimes knock door mirrors out of position, so check them before every journey.

Although the mirrors on modern cars provide an excellent field of view, invariably there are blindspots just behind you on either side. Driving on a motorway gives you a good opportunity to assess blindspots: see how long it takes for a vehicle to appear alongside you after disappearing from your door mirror.

Before changing lanes or overtaking, a glance over your shoulder is a good idea if you suspect a vehicle may be hiding in a blindspot – but make sure the traffic situation ahead makes it safe to do this.

Seat belts

It is compulsory for front and rear passengers to wear seat belts at all times. A driver may unclip the belt while reversing.

Modern inertia-reel seat belts do not normally require adjustment to make them fit comfortably, although some cars provide different positions for the top mounting. Watch out for belts becoming frayed at the edges or twisted in their guides. If your car has old-fashioned static belts, ensure they are always secured tightly.

Children under 3 must be protected by a child safety seat approved by the British Standards Institution. Children aged between 3 and 11 should wear an appropriate child restraint if available, but otherwise they must wear an adult seat belt.

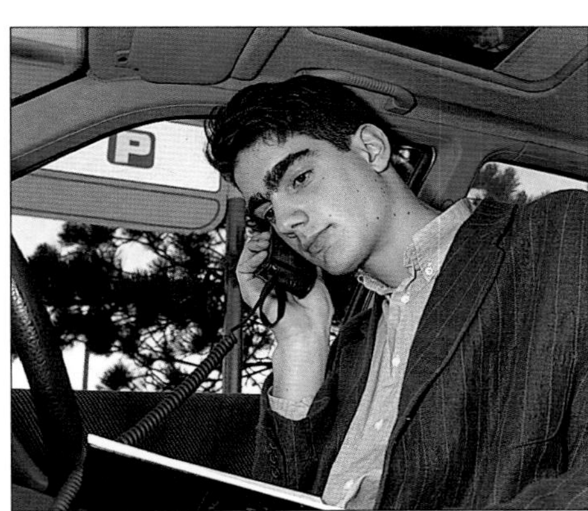

Using a handheld mobile 'phone while driving is illegal–park safely, switch engine off before making a call.

Mobile 'phones

Telephones in cars are a mixed blessing. They are invaluable when a traffic hold-up makes you late, allowing you to let people know and continue your journey with peace of mind. Breakdowns and accidents are other occasions when a mobile 'phone comes into its own.

Although mobile 'phones are helpful only a 'hands-free' installation can safely, and legally, be used while driving, but should only be used sparingly.

A 'phone should be switched off before refuelling to avoid a live electrical circuit in the car.

Keep the interior of your car tidy to avoid distraction from objects rolling around on the floor.

Car clutter

All the things you carry in your car should be packed, stowed and secured properly. A can of drink or a child's toy lying in a footwell becomes an irritating distraction if it rolls around whenever you brake, steer or accelerate.

The rear parcel shelf may seem a convenient place to put a briefcase or a box of cassettes, but such objects can become distracting missiles if you have to brake hard.

Safety checks

Five minutes every week is all it takes to check your car's tyres, lights, fluid levels and windscreen wipers, yet few drivers bother.

Tyre checks are especially important (see page 35). The law requires a minimum tread depth of 1.6mm over the full width of the tyre. Worn or incorrectly inflated tyres are potential killers because grip is reduced, particularly in wet weather.

Advanced checklist

- Adopt a comfortable driving position with hands on the steering wheel at 'ten-to-two' or 'quarter-to-three'.
- Keep mirrors clean and properly adjusted.
- You must always wear seat belts, whether travelling in the front or rear, if they are fitted.
- Always park safely before using a mobile 'phone.
- Keep your car free from clutter and ensure that it is in good working order.

Thinking ahead

Why you need to think ahead

All drivers need to adopt a planned and systematic approach to driving, and this discipline becomes doubly important in congested traffic.

If you concentrate on the conditions around you and anticipate what lies ahead, every manoeuvre can be carried out in good time and under complete control. Experience generally improves a driver's skill in planning actions, but the need to concentrate and anticipate must never be underestimated.

Most accidents occur because a driver fails to identify a hazard soon enough. When danger stares in the face, it may already be too late to avoid an accident. Emergency braking or a sudden swerve may also cause a driver to lose control. Think ahead so that each change of condition is made smoothly and gradually, with the largest possible margin for safety.

Driving plans

At the very heart of the theory of advanced driving technique is the driving plan. How you assess the information before your eyes and how you react to it will distinguish the truly advanced driver from the novice.

The driving plan is based on three questions:

1 What can be seen?
2 What cannot be seen?
3 What may reasonably be expected to happen?

Driving plans must be based on what is actually observed, the assumption that there may be danger in every obscured section of road, and that others may do something foolish at any moment.

It is rare to be able to base your driving plans purely on what you can see because there are nearly always obscured areas. There may be a bend to the right, a blind junction, a hump-back bridge or a high-sided vehicle – any of these can impede your view. Try as you might to extend your view round the hazards, you ultimately have to decide to drive within the limits of what you can see, expecting threats to lurk in those obscured areas.

The third question – what may reasonably be expected to happen? – is the one that catches out the inexperienced driver. It calls for skilful interpretation of the visual clues. Imagine a country B-road bordered by tall hedges. There is an advanced warning triangle for a bend to the left, and ahead you see fresh hedge trimmings along the nearside edge. What do you do?

Well, what can you see? A bend ahead, but you cannot yet see round it. You can see the vegetation in the road, so you can expect a hedge trimmer operating just around the bend, blocking half the road. Before you actually see the obstruction you will have braked to negotiate the bend more slowly than normal, so that you are fully prepared to stop. Other vehicles may be behind, so consider giving an 'I intend to slow down' arm signal.

Similarly, you might be following a commercial vehicle. Make a mental note of what kind it is. If it is a bread van, and you can see shops in the distance, expect it to be making a delivery

A driving plan in the country: long-range observation helps this driver to spot at an early stage the white van parked just round the corner, and a blue car even further ahead – but the hedge is tall enough to conceal an oncoming car approaching the van.

A driving plan in town: good observation well down this 20mph-restricted street gives early notice of an oncoming car about to move into the red car's path, in order to pass two illegally parked vans.

there, possibly without signalling and in the most awkward place.

The same goes for a bus or coach. If you persist in following closely so that you cannot see when a stop is coming up, you may get stuck behind it when it picks up passengers. You will have only yourself to blame. If you stay well back, keeping a look-out for stops and anticipating the inevitability of the bus stopping, you will be ready to overtake as soon as the road is clear.

At night accurate observation is even more important, but different clues are available. Physical clues may be few in the diminished light, but the presence and position of other vehicles may be indicated by their headlights. By day they would not be seen until emerging from that side turning, but at night you receive advanced warning.

When practising your driving plans, never assume anything. Work only with certainties.

These examples of driving plans show how you can anticipate the actions of others. In conjunction with the five-point system which follows (see page 16), driving plans form the basis of advanced driving.

Commentary driving

The IAM has always recommended 'commentary driving' as a useful discipline that should be practised from time to time, although it is no longer an obligatory part of the Advanced Driving Test.

Commentary driving means describing out loud what you observe and what action you take. It gives you a very clear understanding of your anticipation of events and your response to them. You will almost certainly be amazed how much your observation and concentration can be sharpened. Fine-tuning your skills by commentary driving can also add interest to a dull journey.

Your state of mind

Realising the importance of having a clear state of mind is one of the secrets of advanced driving. The pleasure – and sometimes even exhilaration – of driving are rightly savoured by enthusiastic drivers, but these emotions should never come before self-control. Do not allow your enjoyment of driving along a quiet road on a bright spring morning, for example, to cause your speed to creep up unnoticed.

Aggression has no place in advanced driving. Aggressive, incompetent or reckless behaviour from other drivers should also never provoke you. Rise above it and keep yourself out of situations of 'road rage'. Driving with self-control is not only the most satisfying way, but also the safest.

Alcohol is an obvious cause of impaired judgement, but recognise that you are also below your best when tired, stressed or distracted.

A timid approach can be just as dangerous as an aggressive one, for indecision can cause an accident in a situation demanding quick thinking. Good planning and observation, however, always gives you the measure of the situation around you, so occasions when you have to react to the unexpected in a split-second should be very rare.

There are times when it is important to recognise you are not at your best. Extra concentration can be needed on a dull journey over familiar roads, or if you are tired after a bad night's sleep or a long day at work, or even distracted after a row at home. Being delayed in a traffic jam can make you agitated about arriving late. A cold or a mild dose of 'flu can slow your reactions, dull your judgement and make you bad-tempered. Driving under the influence of alcohol or drugs, needless to say, is totally out of the question.

A willingness to learn

You are demonstrating this by studying this book, but are you sure you have an accurate picture of your driving skills? Most of us, advanced drivers included, have too high an opinion of our abilities behind the wheel.

Regardless of your age and experience, there is always more to learn about driving. Never believe that you have reached a plateau of excellence, or that all blame for disconcerting moments on the road should be pinned on others.

Whenever you find yourself guilty of misjudging a situation, even if it is just braking a little too late and heavily for a corner, reflect on it and learn from it. Every journey in your car is an opportunity to improve that little bit further.

Tolerance and courtesy

Take pride in being a tolerant and courteous driver at all times, especially at pedestrian crossings and in traffic. Even the most mild-mannered people become irritated, even angry, when other road users behave stupidly or inconsiderately. Never let your driving standard be affected and remember that your behaviour may act as an example. Resist any temptation to retaliate.

Leaving a convenient gap to allow a vehicle to emerge from a side turning is one example of courteous driving.

Your reaction time

Reaction times vary widely and are invariably longer than you think. A racing driver with naturally fast reactions and fired with adrenalin can react remarkably quickly, in as little as 0.2sec. The average driver is much slower to react: 0.4sec is excellent, 0.5sec is good and 0.8sec is satisfactory. Anything longer than a second is dangerously slow. If your reaction time is 0.5sec, at 70mph you travel 16 metres (about four car lengths) before you respond to a hazard.

To obtain a rough idea of your reaction time, you could go to a driving centre equipped with a simulation tester. As an

Sitting this close behind a lorry leaves this driver with no time to react, let alone stop. At 70mph you travel about four car lengths before you respond to a hazard.

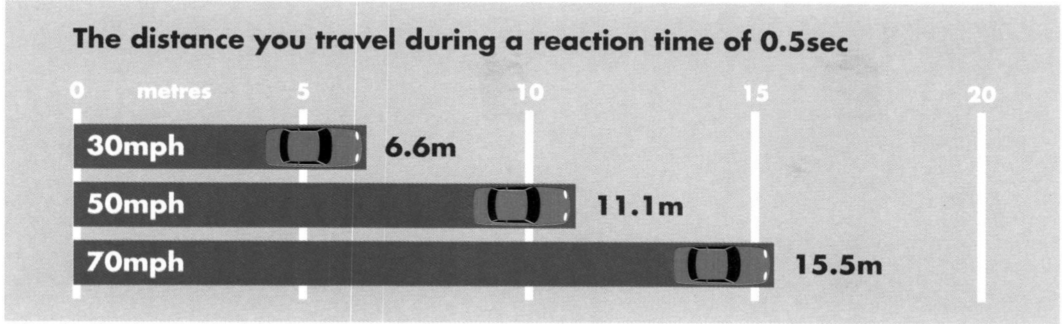

unscientific alternative you could play a party game: someone drops a pencil between your thumb and forefinger, and the speed with which you grip it shows how your reactions compare with other people's.

Your reactions slow down if you are tired, ill, cold or under stress. Alcohol, drugs or prescribed medicines also dramatically impair your reactions.

You reduce the effect of your reaction time by reading the road ahead to observe when and where a hazard might occur. If you suspect danger, move your right foot from the accelerator and hold it poised over the brake pedal. This will save a valuable split-second if you have to take action.

You must allow more reaction time at night because your eyes have to adjust constantly to changing levels of light. The pupil of the eye contracts quickly to adjust your vision when bright lights approach, but takes much longer to adapt to darkness again once the lights have gone.

There is a familiar claim from drivers involved in accidents: 'I stopped dead'. Now you know just how far you can travel while you are reacting to a hazard, you can see that this statement is ridiculous. No vehicle can ever stop 'dead'. If it could, the driver certainly would not stop with it.

Other people's reactions

Always expect slow reactions and poor observation from road users around you. It is common for a driver involved in a collision with another vehicle to complain that its driver 'had plenty of time to see me', and this may be right. But often an accident can be avoided if one driver allows for another's mistakes.

An accident where one car collides with another pulling too slowly across its path could, in some circumstances, be blamed on both parties.

Advanced checklist

- Thinking ahead enables every manoeuvre with your car to be carried out in good time and under complete control.
- Think about driving plans: how you assess information and react to it is a cornerstone of advanced driving technique.
- Regularly practise commentary driving to monitor your powers of observation and anticipation.
- Always drive with self-control and complete concentration.
- Allow for reaction times, your own and those of other road users, when hazards unfold.

What the examiner looks for

- Do you show an awareness of driving plans?
- Do you read the road ahead and react early to hazards?
- Are road and traffic hazards coped with safely and in good time?
- Do you demonstrate the ability to judge speed and distance?
- Do you concentrate properly and avoid distraction?
- Do you show courtesy, especially at pedestrian crossings?
- Do you drive with reasonable restraint, but not indecision?
- Do you follow other vehicles at a safe distance?
- Are your reactions good?

The planned system of driving

A procedure for all hazards

A systematic approach whenever you change speed or course goes hand in hand with the need to think ahead. Scrutiny of accidents shows that in most cases drivers make an error at some point in the sequence, allowing events over which they have no control to overtake them. Although a driver may react wrongly when an instant decision is required, very often the mistake which leads to an accident – perhaps the failure to glance in the mirror or reduce speed soon enough – occurs very early in the sequence.

Whether a hazard is a bend, a junction or just a parked vehicle, the five-point system of control (right) should be used. This is a sequence of actions, although the first phase – Information – overlaps the other four.

Remember that each of these features is to be considered, not slavishly put into action one after the other out of habit. Spelled out in detail this may see long-winded, but in practice it is simple, quick and necessary. The mnemonic 'IPSGA' makes it easy to remember. Practising it time and again will make it almost instinctive.

The system is not rigid: some circumstances call for extra checks in the mirrors before braking, while others require only some parts of the procedure. By imposing this discipline on yourself and thinking well ahead, you will never be caught out by unexpected developments on the road.

This planned method also minimises the danger of other road users being surprised by your actions. 'I didn't know the car was going to turn right and it seemed safe to pass': this familiar excuse from other drivers can never be valid if your intentions are always clear. As well as keeping other road users informed, it is just as important to keep checking they have seen you and are reacting accordingly.

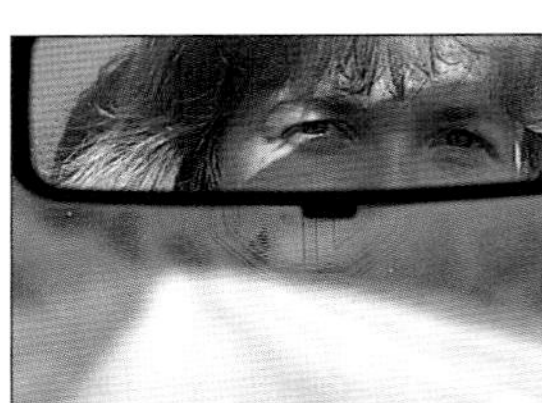

INFORMATION

Take information
Look all round you, using your mirrors to study the situation behind.

Use information
Using what you have observed, plan how to deal with the identified hazards.

Give information
Give a signal if it is helpful to other road users. Use of indicators will be the normal method, but consider arm signals, horn and flashed headlights as necessary.

POSITION
After giving a signal, take up the correct position on the road. You may need to check your mirrors again before changing course.

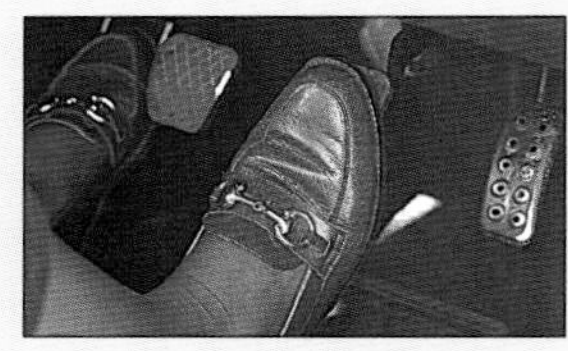

SPEED
Adjust your speed to the correct level for the hazard by using the brakes or engine braking (or the accelerator as necessary). You may need to check your mirrors again.

GEAR
Once travelling at the right speed, select the correct gear. If time is short, you may need to change gear shortly before you finish braking. Consider making a final mirror check.

ACCELERATION
Once your car is on a straight course after the hazard, accelerate to a suitable speed.

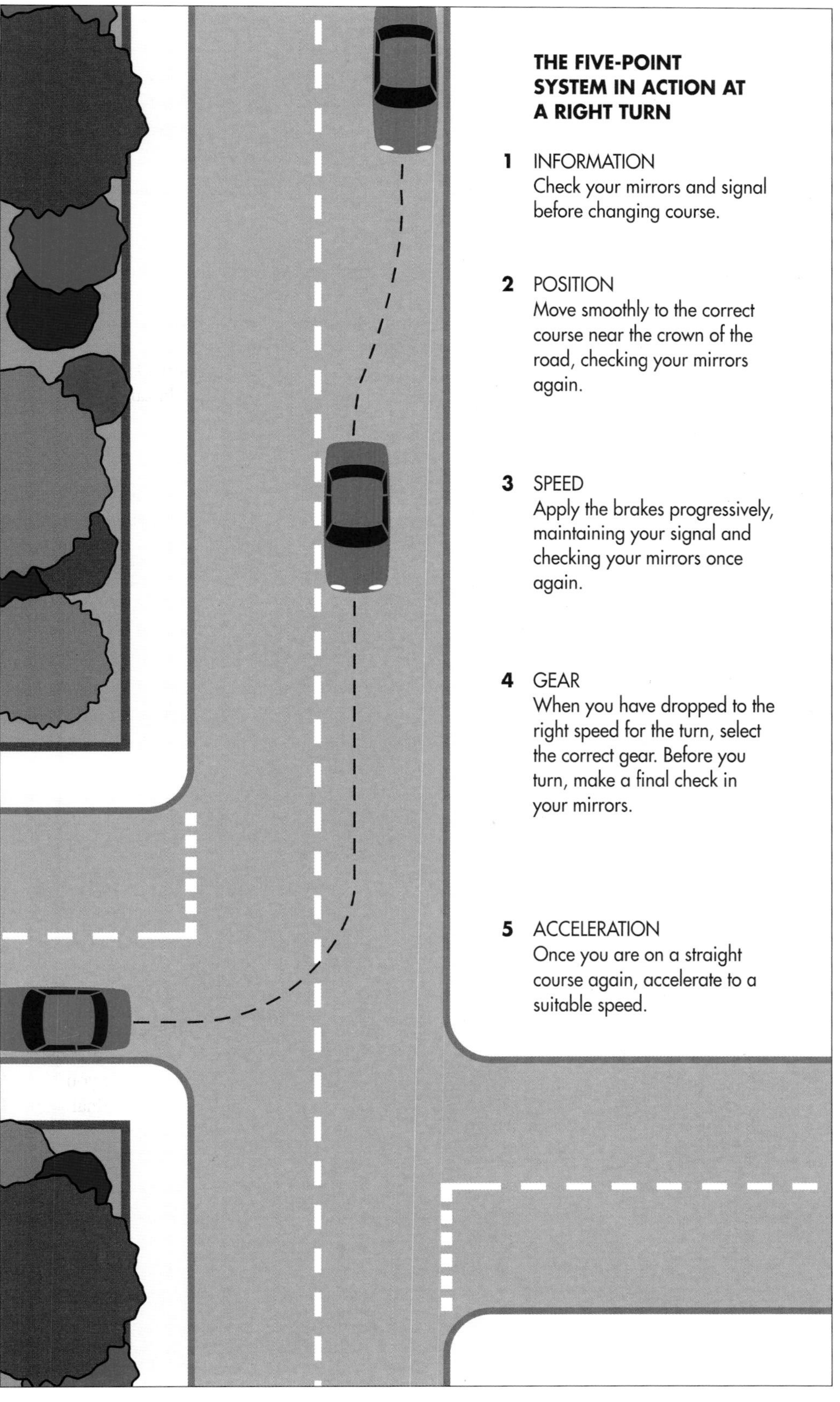

THE FIVE-POINT SYSTEM IN ACTION AT A RIGHT TURN

1 INFORMATION
Check your mirrors and signal before changing course.

2 POSITION
Move smoothly to the correct course near the crown of the road, checking your mirrors again.

3 SPEED
Apply the brakes progressively, maintaining your signal and checking your mirrors once again.

4 GEAR
When you have dropped to the right speed for the turn, select the correct gear. Before you turn, make a final check in your mirrors.

5 ACCELERATION
Once you are on a straight course again, accelerate to a suitable speed.

Advanced checklist

- Absorb the planned system of driving: it is used whenever you want to change speed or course, and forms the basis for advanced driving.
- Remember there are two major reasons for using this method: you are always prepared for unexpected developments, and other road users are never surprised by your actions.

What the examiner looks for

- Do you have a good appreciation of the planned system of driving?
- Are signals given at the right time?
- Is your use of mirrors to a high standard?
- Is the system put into action in good time, avoiding late braking and snatched gearchanges?
- In applying the five-point system, do you seek to avoid any overlap in your braking, gearchanging and steering?

Observation

A basic skill of advanced driving

Good powers of observation, which demand practice, concentration and thought, keep you out of trouble. You need to absorb all the information around you and select what is useful. All drivers do this to a certain extent, but the advanced driver sees far more. Road sense is developed into an art.

Advanced drivers constantly assess the changing road and traffic conditions around them, reading the road a long way ahead and checking behind.

Vision

Make sure your vision is satisfactory. The ability to read a vehicle number plate at 20.5 metres (67ft) is the legal minimum, but good quality observation depends on much better sight than this.

Research has shown that an alarming number of drivers have eyesight deficiencies, yet most remain unaware that anything is wrong. Eyesight usually deteriorates so gradually that someone can have a vision defect and perhaps compensate for it subconsciously. If you try to avoid driving at night because of your vision, you should acknowledge that it might also be less than perfect in daylight.

Eyesight problems affect safety. Having little or no sharp sight in one eye prevents good judgement of distance. Tunnel vision, the tendency to concentrate only on the view directly ahead, seriously restricts powers of observation; good peripheral sight is essential in order to see what is happening to either side. Long sight and short sight are extremely common (and proportionately worse at night), yet many drivers remain unaware of it until forced eventually to have an eye test.

How good is your eyesight? A supermarket car park is a handy place to check how well you can read a number plate – eight parking spaces roughly indicate the legal minimum.

Forward observation

Some inexperienced drivers look at the part of the road immediately in front of them, failing to notice sufficiently early the approach of junctions, roundabouts, traffic slowing down, parked cars and any other potential hazards. You should concentrate your gaze on a point some way ahead, while at the same time taking in events even further in the distance as well as those closer to you and to either side.

This selective vision requires concentration and has to be developed with practice, so train yourself to cast an eye over as wide a field of vision as possible. Peripheral vision can take in a dog on the verge at the same time as you watch an overtaking car in the distance. Your centre of focus must be adjusted constantly according to speed and how far ahead the road is visible.

When you start applying the five-point system (see pages 16-17) you will probably find all you can do is note mentally what you see ahead. After a while you should be able to say what you intend to do about the things you see. For example: 'The car waiting at that junction on the left about 300 metres ahead may pull across my path. The driver is looking at traffic coming the other way, so has he even seen me? I will ease off the accelerator and poise my foot above the brake pedal just in case.'

Good forward observation means looking at the road a long way ahead. An advanced driver spots this exposed bridge, and thinks about its implications, long before the sign can be read.

So many potential hazards occur in town: this driver needs to watch pedestrians appearing from all directions, illegally parked vehicles on the left, the blue van slowing down and indicating, and red traffic lights at the crossroads in the distance.

Keeping your distance

Other vehicles and your position relative to them affect how much you can see. Dropping further back, particularly behind a lorry or van, always enables you to see more of the road and traffic ahead.

Gentle adjustments of your position on the road allow you to maximise your view to either side, and bends in either direction can allow new sight lines to open up. Be aware that corners can also close down parts of your view: through a left-hand bend a group of heavy vehicles ahead of you can temporarily obscure the oncoming traffic stream.

A much better view round a lorry can be obtained by adjusting your road position – in this case by moving towards the centre line – and keeping your distance.

Selective observation

Good observation is essential to advanced driving, but the refinement of this skill comes in learning to be selective in what you observe. In a busy city centre, for example, you need to distinguish what should be acted upon and what can be ignored. Some pointers will give you an idea of the range of visual information which helps you to become a safer driver.

- Allow for any changes in the road surface that will affect grip: mud at farm or building site entrances, patches of wet leaves in autumn and streams of water in wet weather are examples.
- Unexpected movements by parked vehicles must always be allowed for, especially if you can see a driver inside. The vehicle can suddenly move out into your path if the driver sets off without thinking, or someone might open a door.

Telegraph poles can indicate the course of a bend before you actually see it.

- A line of telegraph poles can give early warning of a bend, but remember that occasionally the wires can track straight on while the road bends.
- Give stationary vans a wide berth, especially on quiet roads, in case the driver gets out unexpectedly.
- Always give a cyclist plenty of room. Not all cyclists are skilled on their bicycles, so always expect a wobble. A cyclist might also steer round a pothole or drain as you pass.
- Any parked vehicle can hide a pedestrian about to step out, so look for tell-tale feet visible underneath it; school buses, delivery vans and ice cream vans need particular care.
- Any pedestrian needs to be observed carefully. A child can dash into the road without looking; an old person, perhaps with failing eyesight or hearing, might not see you coming; a dog off a lead could do anything.
- Is the driver of a vehicle waiting at a junction looking in your direction? Watching head and hand movements will help you judge whether the driver has seen you and will stay put until you have passed.
- Be especially alert with pedestrians in wet weather: people hurrying for shelter or keeping their heads down in rain are not always so careful.
- Intelligent observation of other vehicles can give you early warning. A parked car with its reversing lights on is about to move backwards. A vibration or puff of smoke from the exhaust of a parked car means that its driver has just started the engine and may pull into your path.
- Give more room to the aggressive or sloppy driver: drop further back from a driver ahead trying to overtake when there is no opportunity, or a driver who is paying more attention to finding a particular address in town than to the road.
- If you are behind a bus, passengers getting up and moving towards the doors suggest it will shortly be stopping.

Look out for tell-tale feet visible beneath parked vehicles.

- A cloud of smoke from the exhaust of a heavy vehicle climbing a hill towards you tells you that its driver has changed down and will be travelling even more slowly. The vehicle could conceal a car whose driver may be about to attempt a rash overtaking manoeuvre.
- Is the driver of the car ahead of you paying full attention to the road? Someone who is using a mobile 'phone, turning round to tell off children in the back seat or having an animated conversation with a passenger is definitely not concentrating on the job in hand.
- Reflections in a shop window at an urban junction or corner can show you an approaching vehicle before you actually see it.

Reflections in shop windows at sharp corners and junctions can give you early notice of oncoming traffic.

Rear observation

Looking in the mirrors is one thing, but observing is quite another. Unskilled drivers obtain only the most basic information from their mirrors: is there a vehicle right behind? You see these people on any motorway or dual-carriageway, their hesitant, sometimes obstructive, driving showing that they have no clue about the broad traffic pattern behind them.

Your mirrors should be used to study the speed and distance of vehicles behind over a long range, just as you observe the road ahead. You do not have to dwell on the view by taking your eyes off the road ahead for a long time – useful information is taken in at a glance.

You will always make your rear-view checks when the situation ahead is safe, giving extra thought to their timing when traffic and road conditions ahead are changing quickly. There is no need to look in the mirrors with over-zealous frequency: your aim is to have total awareness of the position and speed of any vehicles which will affect you.

Supplement your use of the interior mirror with the door mirrors as necessary. If a certain manoeuvre, such as joining a motorway or changing lanes to overtake, leaves you unsure about the situation in mirror blindspots, glance over your shoulder to check – a motorcyclist would call this the 'lifesaver'.

Road signs

Anyone who has passed the L-test should know all road signs, but it is still worth referring to the *Highway Code* periodically to check that you remember all the warning signs (triangular), advisory signs (rectangular) and mandatory signs (circular).

British roads are quite well provided with signs, and all of them are erected for a purpose. You should know at a glance what any sign is telling you and react if necessary. Warning of a school, for example, demands extra caution at times of day when you can expect lots of children, cars and buses to be milling around.

Do not fall into the habit of ignoring signs except when you are searching for particular information. All of them help the advanced driver in the process of thinking ahead.

A pole carrying two or more warning signs should be read from the top. Two triangles with a left-hand bend sign above a junction sign tell you that the bend comes first – so you can infer that the junction might appear quite suddenly.

Unofficial road signs such as 'Gymkhana' or 'Car Boot Sale' provide useful information and help you anticipate. RAC or AA notices of big spectator events may even make you consider finding another route to avoid congested conditions.

A pair of signs should be read from the top. The junction comes after the bend, so it may loom quickly.

Advanced checklist

- Observation depends upon good eyesight, so make sure you have had your eyes tested recently, even if you are confident that your vision has not deteriorated.
- Concentrate your gaze on a point some way ahead, while at the same time taking in events even further in the distance, closer to you and on either side.
- Use your mirrors for long-range observation, so that you always know the speed and distance of vehicles travelling in station with you or closing from a long way behind.
- Develop the skills of selective observation so that you have an eye for any situation which might require action.
- Take in all road signs: their information is always useful to the advanced driver.

What the examiner looks for

- Do you read the road ahead and show a good sense of anticipation?
- Do you demonstrate the ability to judge speed and distance accurately?
- Do you react early enough to hazards?
- Are signals, signs and road markings observed, obeyed and approached correctly?
- Do you use the mirrors intelligently and with suitable frequency?
- Are mirrors used properly in conjunction with signalling and before changing speed or course?

2 ADVANCED CAR CONTROL

Steering

Feeding the wheel

You should hold the steering wheel with your hands at the 'quarter-to-three' or 'ten-to-two' position. Steering movements should be made by feeding the wheel through your hands. The photographs show how the technique works when turning right. You 'pass' the wheel from one hand to the other at all times.

It sounds complicated, but this is the smoothest, safest and most natural way to control the steering. If you are not used to steering in this way, your movements may at first feel they lack co-ordination. But it only takes practice to develop the technique into a fluid, controlled movement. Once perfected, you will find it uncomfortable to steer in any other way.

Anyone who claims this to be an awkward technique is usually making one basic mistake. Whichever way you turn, you always start with a 'pull' from the top rather than a 'push' from the bottom. If you have been tending to push first, practise pulling first and you will notice an almost miraculous improvement in the smoothness and control of your steering.

There are three advantages in feeding the wheel. First, neither hand strays beyond the '12 o'clock' or '6 o'clock' positions, something which greatly reduces the degree of fine control you have over the steering. Second, you have firm control of the steering wheel at all times, with one hand always gripping the wheel tightly while the other holds it loosely. Third, your hands always remain opposite each other in a position where they can instantly steer in either direction, allowing you to react swiftly and with complete control in an emergency.

1 Move your right hand towards the top of the wheel, tighten your grip with it and then pull this hand downwards, letting the wheel slide through the loose grip of your left hand.

2 As your right hand reaches the bottom of the natural arc, slide your left hand down towards it and change your grip to,this hand.

3 Then bring your left hand, now gripping the wheel, upwards so that you keep the wheel moving in a continuous turn. At the same time move your right hand back towards the top of the wheel if you need to apply more lock.

Incorrect styles of steering

There are many ways in which ordinary drivers compromise their steering control. As you read this section, think whether any of these mistakes apply to you. If bad habits have become ingrained, it takes good concentration and repeated practice to eliminate them.

Driving with one hand on the wheel arises simply through laziness. This gives you poor control at all times, and puts you at a disadvantage if you need to react quickly. If, on a long drive, you find it tiring to keep both hands in the correct place, your driving position (see page 10) needs adjustment.

There are many times, of course, when one hand has to be taken off the wheel. Apart from changing gear, opening a window or operating switches are common occasions. Try to do these things when travelling in a straight line and in quiet traffic situations.

If you regularly change gear while steering through junctions or sharp bends, work harder at the five-point system of control (pages 16-17) so that you make time for changing gear after you brake and before you steer. Where it is difficult to make time for these actions in sequence, it is usually best to overlap a gearchange with braking rather than steering.

Many people let go of the wheel completely for brief moments. How can they react if they have to take avoiding action? A common mistake after a turn is to let the steering's self-centring action spin the wheel straight. While doing this, a driver has no control.

Some people hold the wheel with both hands close together at top or bottom. This is neither relaxing nor appropriate for good control. Your hands should be opposite each other to allow quick steering in either direction.

Except when requiring extra leverage when parking or during reversing, crossing arms must be avoided. Control is sacrificed, since crossed arms prevent more lock being added. Imagine you misjudge a corner and halfway through you find it tightening unexpectedly. If your arms are already crossed, you prevent yourself steering any further without a great deal of flapping at the wheel.

Steering accurately

Many drivers do not take the trouble to develop good judgement of the width of their cars. They seem to spend their entire driving careers imagining that their cars are actually a metre wider than they really are. They hold up traffic around them and make slow progress.

The faults of this type of driver affect other road users: waiting until there is room to take an unnecessarily wide course around an obstruction such as a stationary vehicle; failing to tuck properly into the nearside when approaching another vehicle in a narrow lane; refusing to slip through the narrow gap alongside a vehicle waiting to turn right, all the time oblivious to the long queue building up behind.

Work on your steering judgement if this sounds like you. Acquiring a precise idea of your car's width and length enables you to negotiate a path through congested traffic more easily, or to squeeze into a tight parking spot which once would have looked too small.

You can learn to steer more accurately and judge the dimensions of your car by practising in an empty car park on a Sunday morning. Look at your car and mentally form a picture of its precise size. With most cars you are unable to see the extremities from the driving seat, so familiarising yourself with the length of bonnet and tail will help enormously.

Making good progress through urban traffic requires accurate steering and good judgement of your car's dimensions.

Steering for smoothness

The typical driver with coarse steering technique turns the wheel too sharply and causes the car to change direction with a lurch. The advanced driver, however, uses a very subtle progression of steering movement.

Initially the wheel is turned very gently, and then the rate of rotation is slightly speeded up once the car has settled into its cornering attitude. Applying this sensitivity means that passengers hardly feel changes of direction, even at a decent speed. The steering is straightened again after a corner with the same progressive movement.

Timid or inexperienced drivers have a tendency to grip the steering wheel too tightly because of their inability to relax. Apart from being tiring, an excessively strong grip also tends to make steering movements coarser.

On the other hand, the over-confident driver who treats the steering wheel as if it were the only remaining egg of a recently extinct bird of prey could get into trouble if a swift avoiding manoeuvre has to be made.

Steering should be applied progressively, and the hands should be moved in good time to the required position for feeding the wheel.

Steering messages

Messages through the steering wheel about how the front wheels are reacting to the road surface give the experienced driver a good deal of useful, and sometimes vital, information. Sensitivity in steering provides early warning of when the tyres are beginning to lose grip, particularly in slippery conditions.

On a car with power-assisted steering, the driver may be denied some of this all-important steering feel. Although many modern power steering systems vary the level of assistance according to speed, feedback from the front wheels can still be masked.

Power steering must be treated with respect because it is all too easy for sudden steering movement on a slippery road to cause the front wheels to break grip and start a skid. Artificial lightness should not be regarded as an indication that a car's roadholding is any better.

Basic handling characteristics

You do not need vast technical and engineering knowledge to appreciate and react to the basic handling characteristics of a car. Roadholding and handling behaviour depend on the design of the suspension, the position of the engine, the type of tyres fitted and the position of the driving wheels.

A few cars, but not many, possess completely neutral handling characteristics. Most have a tendency to oversteer or understeer. These terms refer to the in-built tendencies of the car, and have nothing to do with actions taken by the driver.

Front-wheel drive cars tend to need more steering lock than you expect to hold course through a bend, especially at higher speeds – this is understeer. Rear-wheel drive cars tend to need less steering lock than you expect, requiring you to ease off the steering slightly to keep the car on course – this is oversteer. The 'under' and 'over' refer to how the car responds to steering deflection.

Advanced checklist

- Always steer by feeding the steering wheel through your hands, so that you have at least one hand gripping the wheel at all times.
- Start all steering movements with a 'pull' from the top of the wheel, not a 'push' from the bottom.
- Learn to steer accurately, with a clear idea of your car's width.
- Steer with progressive movements of the hands; coarse steering can cause the front wheels to skid in slippery conditions.
- Hold the steering wheel with a gentle but firm touch, for maximum sensitivity.

What the examiner looks for

- Is the steering wheel held correctly, with the hands at the 'quarter-to-three' or 'ten-to-two' positions?
- Do you pass the wheel through your hands?
- Is use of the 'cross-arms' technique confined to manoeuvring?
- Do you steer smoothly and accurately?
- Do you ever let go of the wheel altogether?
- Do you position your car properly?

Using the gears

Transmission types

Almost all modern cars with manual gearboxes have five speeds.

Most people choose to drive a car fitted with a manual gearbox not just because it is cheaper. On the whole, a manual gearchange offers a greater degree of control, and comes with a choice of four, five or even six forward gears.

Automatics usually come with three or four forward speeds, and, of course, no clutch is fitted. Most automatics offer some degree of manual control, but some, such as the 'Tiptronic' system developed by Porsche, provide a choice between a conventional automatic mode and completely manual operation. With this type of transmission, the driver can select each gear electronically by moving a conventional lever or by pressing a button on the steering wheel.

A different type of automatic gearbox is the simple-to-use Constantly Variable Transmission (CVT). This merely requires the driver to choose the direction of travel by pushing the lever forwards or backwards.

A few high-performance cars, such as this BMW M5, have six-speed gearboxes.

Smooth use of gears and clutch

Good gearchanges, whether up or down, are accomplished unnoticed by your passengers. To use the gearbox really well, it is necessary to match gears, road speed and engine speed, and to use the clutch and accelerator pedals skilfully. Poor gearchanging will give your passengers an uncomfortable ride and put unnecessary strain on the engine and transmission.

Some race driving schools use a clever method to encourage smooth driving. A large saucer is attached to the bonnet of a car and a heavy ball, something like snooker ball, is allowed to roll freely in it. The pupil has to use all the controls smoothly so that the ball does not roll out with gearchanges, acceleration, braking or turns into corners. Imagine you are being put through the same test on public roads and try to drive smoothly enough to avoid 'losing the ball'. If your passengers' heads bob backwards and forwards with each gearchange, you could do a great deal better.

When changing up, you should release the accelerator completely and only press it again when the clutch has re-engaged, timing these movements accurately so that you maintain smooth progress. When changing down, however, it is best to maintain a little pressure on the accelerator as you select the lower gear, so that engine speed has become matched to road speed when you engage the clutch.

Accurately co-ordinated gearchanges give your car's clutch a much longer life. Poor drivers commonly press the accelerator too early during a gearchange, causing strain on the clutch when it is forced to slip as the pedal is brought up. Other faults that can quickly wear out a clutch are using excessive revs when pulling away from standstill and driving with the left foot resting on the pedal.

Choosing the correct gear

You should achieve a balance between economy, performance and mechanical sympathy when choosing which gear to be in. Some drivers seem determined to reach top gear as soon as possible and stay there irrespective of the road conditions ahead, while others hold intermediate gears for so long that the engine races away at high revs. Striking a balance between the two is obviously the best way to drive.

When moving away from rest, always use first gear. Some drivers pull away in second, which strains the transmission and engine, and makes it more difficult to deal with a situation where the extra acceleration offered by first gear is needed instantly.

You should make the fullest use of the gearbox on occasions when a lower gear would be better, such as overtaking or climbing hills. A low gear should always be used for maximum engine braking when driving down a steep hill. Generally the gear you select to drive up a particular hill should be the same one that you use to descend it.

In normal driving you change up through the gears in sequence, but this does not need to be a hard-and-fast rule. If, for example, you find yourself in a situation, such as overtaking, where you need to take the engine to high revs in third gear, it can be appropriate to omit fourth gear and go straight to fifth when you settle down to a cruising speed. This is called 'block' gearchanging. However, you should always be sure when doing this that you remain in the right gear for the conditions.

'Block' gearchanging is far more commonly used when slowing down (see 'Gears or brakes?'). When you approach a junction or sharp bend, you use the brakes to slow down and then select the right gear when you have finished braking. This often means that you omit several intermediate gears.

On an open road, for example, you may be travelling in fifth gear when you start preparing to turn left. You will slow down with the brakes and then select the appropriate gear, perhaps second, to make the turn and accelerate away again.

If a rev counter is fitted, it can be a useful aid in deciding when to change gear.

Gears or brakes?

Many drivers go down through the gears in sequence during braking for a low-speed hazard, such as a junction, roundabout or sharp corner, but this is not the way an advanced driver slows down.

Long ago, when brakes were far less efficient, 'sequential downchanging' provided a useful engine-braking effect, but slowing down in a modern car should be achieved with brakes alone, except when descending a steep hill, on icy surfaces (see page 58), or in an emergency caused by brake failure.

It is cheaper to wear out brake pads rather than the gearbox. Every modern car can lock its brakes if the pedal is stamped hard enough, so in normal conditions there is simply no need to supplement use of the brakes with down-through-the-gears engine braking. Since tyre adhesion determines how smartly your car can stop, you can see that use of brakes alone is sufficient.

Changing gear while braking should, under normal circumstances, be avoided. However there are occasions when it is appropriate, and beneficial, to partially overlap braking and changing gear, provided that it is planned and executed with finesse in a balanced and unhurried way. Poor observations can result in a hurried and unplanned overlap of braking and changing gear that, in turn, affects the smoothness of the drive, which is unacceptable for the purpose of the IAM test.

Slowing down is normally achieved with the brakes alone, but changing to a lower gear is wise when descending a steep hill.

Using good anticipation and observation, you will use the brakes in good time when you approach a hazard, then select the right gear. Generally the gearchange will be made after braking but before you need to turn the steering wheel.

Double declutching

This technique, a prerequisite before the days of synchromesh gearboxes, is not normally necessary these days, but it could be useful when driving a classic car or a more recent car with worn synchromesh.

Double declutching enables you to select gears without grating their teeth. Quickly bring up the clutch pedal while the gear lever is in neutral and press it down again before you select the next gear. When changing up, keep your foot off the accelerator. When changing down, build up the revs while the clutch is briefly engaged in order to match engine speed to the lower gear.

Coming to a stop

The technique you use when coming to a complete halt after driving along in one of the higher gears often causes problems for candidates during the Advanced Driving Test. What you should do is best illustrated by imagining you are travelling along a suburban road in fifth gear at 40mph and traffic lights ahead turn red.

You slow down your car on the brakes alone, but there comes a point when the engine starts to labour. This is the moment when you de-clutch progressively, in order to prevent the engine straining the transmission and ultimately stalling. Normally it is a rule of advanced driving that you should not 'coast' with the clutch disengaged or the gearbox in neutral, but in this case you have to break this rule briefly by de-clutching so that you come to a halt without stalling the engine.

Never change into neutral before you have stopped and first secured the car on the handbrake. Engage first gear again shortly before you expect to move off.

Using an automatic

The biggest advantage of automatic transmission is that it allows you to keep both hands on the steering wheel whenever your car is moving. The concentration you normally devote to changing gear can instead be focused on the road.

When you need brisk acceleration, the 'kickdown' facility provides it by engaging a lower gear if you push the accelerator pedal smartly.

The main drawback of an automatic is that its torque converter can cause acceleration to be slower. Occasions arise when the driver's judgement is superior, so 'hold' positions for the intermediate ratios are available on the selector lever. If you want maximum acceleration to the engine's limit, it can be better to control the selector lever yourself to avoid the slight pause in progress produced by an automatic change.

Unless you hold the car on the handbrake, or, for a brief stop, on the brake pedal, it will creep at engine tickover with the selector in 'D' (Drive) or 'R' (Reverse). When stationary in traffic, even for many minutes, it is not necessary to move the lever into neutral because the torque converter absorbs most of the engine's propulsion force – no wear occurs. In fact more wear takes place when the driver moves the lever from neutral into a gear.

Always ensure your foot is kept clear of the accelerator when selecting 'D' or 'R' from stationary, in order to avoid take-off being faster than you bargain for.

An automatic may seem strange when you first handle one, if you have become accustomed to a manual, so be very cautious until you are used to it. Never use your left foot on the brake pedal just because you have nothing else to do with it – your feet could become mixed up in an emergency.

If you pass your L-test in an automatic, you will be restricted to this kind of car. Take another test at the earliest opportunity in a car with a manual gearbox so that you can drive any car.

Advanced checklist

- Gearchanges should be made so smoothly and precisely that passengers do not notice them; smooth downward changes require a little pressure on the accelerator pedal to match engine speed to road speed when drive is taken up again.
- Correct use of gears is a basic requirement of advanced driving; use the intermediate ratios whenever they are necessary, including for brisk acceleration.
- Do not change down through the gears during normal slowing down, except in an emergency; the brakes are designed for this purpose.
- Use the lower gears for maximum engine braking down a steep hill, on a slippery road in conditions that might lead to skidding, or if your car's brakes fail.
- Automatic gearboxes remove the need for decision-making about gearchanges in normal driving conditions, but consider using the intermediate 'hold' positions when brisk acceleration is needed.
- Consider your gearchanging to be sufficiently smooth only if your passengers remain perfectly still when you make upward or downward shifts.

What the examiner looks for

- Are engine and road speeds properly co-ordinated when changing gear, especially during down-changes?
- Do you slip or ride the clutch?
- Except when coming to a complete stop, do you ever coast with the clutch disengaged?
- Is your change action smooth, without jerking?
- Are the gears correctly selected and used?
- Is the right gear selected before reaching a hazard?
- If your car has automatic transmission, do you make full use of it, with proper appreciation of the intermediate 'holds'?
- Is a lower gear selected after braking is completed?

Acceleration and speed

Using power wisely

Even the least powerful cars available today can reach high speeds very quickly, but no car should ever have its performance abused. Constantly pushing your car hard in low gears just because it seems like fun is not skilled driving. Power should always be used wisely.

There are many occasions, such as overtaking or blending with traffic from a slip road, when strong acceleration is required. If a slower vehicle on a dual-carriageway starts to move into your lane just as you are passing it, accelerating out of trouble may be better than braking. It is just as important, though, to recognise the circumstances when acceleration should be used with restraint.

You need to develop an instinctive understanding of how to obtain maximum response from your engine, by being in the right gear at the right time. Pressing the accelerator when travelling in a high gear at relatively low speed will do little except increase fuel consumption and exhaust pollution. Judging the part of the rev band that gives the best acceleration comes with familiarity and experience.

Fast getaways in a front-wheel drive car can induce instability if the driving wheels briefly break traction – notice the strip of rubber that has been laid here.

If you want to explore the capabilities of your car, find a deserted stretch of road and put it through its paces up to the speed limit. Use the rev counter – or the gearchange markers on the speedometer – to help you explore the limits of the upper rev ranges. Alternatively, you could consider joining one of the car clubs which hold test days for its members on a variety of racing circuits for this very purpose. After suitable tuition you can enjoy your car's performance at higher speeds than the law permits on public roads.

In using firm acceleration, you also need to have an awareness of its effect on your car's driving wheels.

A front-wheel drive car will lose grip quickly under hard acceleration, particularly in wet or slippery conditions, because of weight transfer from front to rear. Pulling away too smartly from rest, for example, can induce wheelspin, even on a dry surface.

Weight transfer means that rear-wheel drive cars gain extra grip on the driving wheels, as long as acceleration is not excessive. If your car is mid-engined or rear-engined, available grip will be improved still further.

Four-wheel drive vehicles generally have superior grip under acceleration, irrespective of engine position. However, the various types of four-wheel drive transmission differ in how they distribute power between the front and rear axles.

Acceleration sense

Developing advanced sensitivity in varying your speed with the accelerator to suit ever-changing traffic conditions is a vital element of advanced driving, and relies on anticipation, observation and good judgement of speed and distance.

Time accelerator, gearchange and clutch actions accurately to achieve smooth progress through the gears. Snatched gearchanges and on-off use of the accelerator may get you up the road a whisker more quickly, but your car will dive and squat with each change, you will cause unnecessary wear to the transmission, the driving wheels might briefly break traction, and passengers will find the ride uncomfortable.

You should use the accelerator with controlled, progressive movements. When you want decent acceleration, apply the accelerator gently at first to avoid suddenly changing the car's pitch, then increase the pressure once the car feels settled. Use the

Fine-tuning your sense of speed brings precision to your driving. When you see a lower speed limit in the distance, come off the power at a point which allows you to drop to the exact speed, using engine braking alone, the moment you pass the sign.

same approach when coming off the power, by easing your foot back gradually. Your right foot should always alter the power with a gentle flexing movement, not a jerk.

Fine-tuning your acceleration sense adds interest and pleasure to any journey, and leads to much less use of the brakes. On a twisty country road, judge the precise point to stop accelerating after a bend so that engine braking alone brings you down to the right speed for the next corner. Do the same when closing in on a slower vehicle: come off the throttle at the point that allows your car to home in neatly towards the safe following distance without using the brakes. Use this technique when you see a speed limit sign in the distance, so that you drop to the exact speed the moment you pass the sign. Refining your acceleration sense in these ways can give you great pride in the precision of your driving.

Acceleration and overtaking

Normally you will have no need to push your car to its limits when overtaking, as each manoeuvre will be accomplished at a speed that is safe and reasonable.

If you find yourself forcing the engine to strain every sinew, you are attempting to overtake with an insufficient safety margin. Always select the correct gear before you make your first move to overtake.

You should time your actions so that changing up a gear can be delayed until you have returned safely to the left-hand side of the road. Releasing the clutch in a hurry can make your car unstable, and any pause in acceleration obviously means that you spend more time on the 'wrong' side of the road. If you must change up while overtaking, do so swiftly but smoothly.

Use the best gear for strong acceleration when overtaking, and judge your move so that you avoid having to change gear before you return to the left-hand side of the road.

Accelerating on bends

An advanced driver should try to ensure that acceleration is used generally when the front wheels are pointing straight ahead, particularly when brisk acceleration is needed. Applying too much power when the front wheels are turned can upset the car's balance.

There are occasions when acceleration in a bend is unavoidable, or even desirable, but it must be used with care. Acceleration may not be critical to your car's handling at low speeds, but even a little throttle movement at high speeds may impose too great a load on the tyres and compromise grip. With a front-wheel drive car, excessive acceleration will make the front wheels run wide, a condition known as 'understeer' (see page 24).

When you turn into a bend, your car naturally scrubs off some speed. To maintain speed it is necessary to apply a little more pressure on the accelerator. Properly judged, this technique improves your car's stability and the smoothness of your steering, but it should not cause your car to increase speed.

Speed

Speed limits should not be taken at face value, since some situations require a slower pace. It could be legal to travel at 30mph along a residential road, but a child running suddenly into your path would have little chance. Traffic calming measures exist because so many drivers are unable to keep down to a safe speed.

Speed limits must be obeyed and any breach of the law during your Advanced Driving Test will result in failure. The discipline you need for the test must be applied to all of your driving, even if you think there are occasions when a higher speed is safe.

It may be tempting to wind your speed a little higher than 60mph on an open two-way road with wide verges, excellent visibility, no traffic and no side turnings, but remember that you cannot enjoy advanced driving if you lose your licence. Without concentration, indeed, you can find your speed creeping up in good driving conditions without your noticing.

A basic rule of advanced driving is that you should travel at a speed which allows you to stop within the distance you can see. Be especially aware of this rule on familiar roads, where your local knowledge can tempt you to drive faster than is safe.

Speed restrictions are limits, not targets. Many roads allow you legally to travel at speeds which frankly are not safe, so you use good judgement at all times. Main roads in rural areas sometimes permit you to pass through a straggle of houses at 60mph, a speed which would prevent you stopping in time if a child or a dog ran out of a concealed driveway. On a busy high street it could be reckless to drive at more than 15mph, even though double this speed may be legal.

Excessive speed has a huge impact on safety. Research has shown that people who drive fast regardless of their surroundings are between three and five times more likely to have an accident. It is not just your own safety that is affected: a pedestrian hit by a car travelling at 20mph is likely to survive, but someone hit at 40mph is almost certain to be killed.

Driving well below a speed limit, however, can cause frustration if you hold up traffic, inviting impetuous drivers to pass you unsafely. On busy suburban roads you can even encounter pressure from drivers behind when observance of a limit means you travel more slowly than the flow. But always avoid being pressured into breaking the limit.

Warming the engine

Mechanical sympathy means you should avoid using strong acceleration until your car's engine and gearbox have warmed up, unless you need to take emergency action. Revving to 6000rpm before the oil is warm will significantly shorten the engine's life, and there is a case for saying that you, the driver, also need to get into the swing of things before easing your speed higher.

Modern engines with fuel injection tend not to suffer flat-spots and hesitancy even when cold, but an engine with carburettors might give unreliable acceleration while it is warming up, especially if you have to manipulate a manual choke. Remember this when pulling away from junctions in your first few miles on a cold morning, and avoid overtaking until you are certain the engine is performing cleanly.

Advanced checklist

- Familiarise yourself with your car's acceleration capabilities, but use all of the available power only when absolutely necessary.
- Develop your acceleration sense. You will know instinctively when a manoeuvre, such as overtaking, can be carried out safely, and you will find that you use the brakes less.
- Use as much power (in the most suitable gear) as seems safe and reasonable when overtaking.
- Use the accelerator smoothly and progressively, not with sudden movements.
- Remember when cornering that pressure on the accelerator should be used only to maintain speed, not to increase it.

What the examiner looks for

- Is acceleration smooth and progressive?
- Is use of acceleration excessive or insufficient?
- Is acceleration used at the right time and place?
- Are speed limits always observed?
- Bearing in mind road, traffic and weather conditions, do you keep up a reasonable pace and maintain good progress?

Braking

Developing smoothness in braking

You should always use your car's brakes smoothly and progressively. Good use of the brakes requires observation and anticipation, so that you begin your braking at an early stage and always leave a decent margin for braking more heavily if the need arises.

As with the rest of the controls, the advanced driver develops a subtle technique on the brake pedal. Pressure is 'rolled' progressively on and progressively off at each end of the braking period, most of the slowing down occurring through the middle phase. The best way to practise this is to imagine that you want to bring your car to a stop in a normal distance without your passengers noticing.

Braking in good time and with progression allows a good safety margin. Here, for example, braking too late and too hard could cause problems with reduced grip on a cattle grid so close to a junction.

You will ease on to the brake pedal so imperceptibly that no sudden dip of the car's nose can be detected. Increasing the pressure smoothly will then brush off most of your speed, and at the right moment you will bring your foot off the pedal with the same progression. If you are braking to a complete halt at a junction or in traffic, delicate withdrawal of pressure from the pedal will allow your car to roll gently to a standstill, with no dip of the nose.

Always aim to carry out braking with a single, sustained use of the pedal and with your maximum braking occurring through that middle phase. Approaching a roundabout, for example, you will assess the right moment to begin braking, judging the intensity of braking so that you arrive just when a gap in the traffic flow opens up. This precision during approach requires concentration and good timing, so tell yourself to try harder if you start braking too late, if you find yourself having to increase pedal pressure right at the end of your braking, or if you go onto the brakes more than once.

Following the five-point system of control (see page 16) means that you finish your braking before selecting the correct gear for your reduced speed. If poor planning or traffic conditions ever mean that you lack time to brake, change gear and steer in the proper sequence, your chosen compromise should be to overlap the gearchange with your braking. This is safer than trying to change gear while steering.

Most drivers brake too late and too hard. The advanced driver spreads out braking over a longer distance, but not so exaggeratedly that progress is slower.

Braking distance

The distance you need to stop your car is a combination of thinking distance and stopping distance. Thinking distance depends on your speed of reaction (see page 15). Stopping distance depends on the road surface and the efficiency of your car's brakes and tyres. As a general rule, however, remember the stopping distances given in the *Highway Code*:

23 metres (75ft) from 30mph
53 metres (175ft) from 50mph
96 metres (315ft) from 70mph

As a general rule of thumb, stopping distance quadruples when speed doubles. The higher the speed, the more likely a driver is to leave insufficient stopping distance. Remember also that braking distances are significantly increased in wet weather. If you are unsure about how far 96 metres (the stopping distance at 70mph) looks, the white marker posts along the edge of motorways and some dual-carriageways are an ideal guide – they are placed at 100-metre intervals.

A typical motorway scene: drivers travelling with complete disregard for safe stopping distances.

On a fast road an estimate of time gives a good idea of safe braking distance. In dry weather a gap of two seconds will ensure that you can brake safely to rest from 60mph if the car in front stops suddenly.

Brake in a straight line

Because braking has a significant effect on steering, it is always best to ensure that you finish braking before reaching a bend. Using the brakes in the middle of a bend upsets a car's balance and handling characteristics.

There are circumstances, however, when even the most careful driver will need to brake in a bend. An unexpected obstacle in the road such as a horse rider, stray sheep or a tree branch will require swift action, but the brakes must be applied progressively to avoid locking the wheels.

Note the absence of brake lights: approaching a corner, braking should be completed before steering into it.

A car with locked wheels cannot stop at anywhere near the best possible rate, whether travelling through a corner or in a straight line. Since the most powerful braking occurs just before the wheels lock up, it is useful to develop a feel for this moment. A skidpan or disused airfield are suitable places to practise emergency braking.

In the absence of an unexpected hazard, sudden braking in a corner always results from poor observation and anticipation. An advanced driver brakes in a bend only in an emergency.

Cadence braking

Locking the wheels is always a danger in an emergency stop. If this occurs, you will not have full control of your car's steering and you will not slow down quickly enough.

An expert driver deals with locked brakes by using a pulsing technique – 'cadence' braking – that keeps the wheels rolling for optimum braking in an emergency stop. This is how cadence braking works.

When the driver feels one or more wheels begin to lock, pressure on the brake pedal is momentarily released to allow the locked wheels to rotate again, then the pedal is immediately pressed hard again for maximum stopping power. The foot is moved on and off the brake pedal in a split-second for maximum effect. The process may need to be repeated several times to bring the car to rest.

With practice, this on-off technique can be refined to the point where the wheels are kept almost continuously gripping at the threshold of lock-up, the point at which a car stops most efficiently. Cadence braking also allows a fair degree of steering control.

Naturally, it is better never to get yourself into a situation that requires use of cadence braking, but in an emergency, on a slippery surface for example, this technique could avoid an accident.

The real experts in cadence braking are rally drivers who time their hard pushes on the brake pedal to coincide with the spring frequency of the front suspension, thereby taking advantage of the car's inclination to nose-dive. Heavy braking pushes a car down on its front springs and increases the weight on the front tyres, usefully improving their grip. When the brake is released during cadence braking, the front of the car lifts momentarily.

With perfect timing, this bouncing action can be exploited, and even deliberately exaggerated, to gain a useful increase in front tyre adhesion. Obviously this technique is highly specialised, suitable only after considerable private practice, and appropriate on the road only in dire emergency.

The essential thing is to remember that the brakes stop the wheels, but that the tyres stop the car. You should be totally familiar with your car's braking capabilities, and have a highly developed awareness of the limits of adhesion on all kinds of road surfaces.

Anti-lock brakes

Anti-lock brakes, also known as ABS, in effect do cadence braking for you, although considerably more quickly and efficiently than any driver could manage. Sensors and pressure-limiting valves, controlled by a computer, do the combined work of the foot and brain, their operation being felt as pulses through the pedal.

This technical advance is a valuable safety aid, although no driver of a car fitted with ABS should be lulled into a false sense of security, or abuse the system by relying on it to make faster progress in poor conditions. Any advanced driver ought to be able to drive for several years without calling upon a car's ABS.

Brake failure

Check the brakes every time you get into your car. Before pulling away from rest, operate the handbrake down and up to be certain of firm grip, and check that the brake pedal moves efficiently and gives a good feel. Once on the move, try the brakes as soon as you can to be sure they work properly.

Since most modern cars have dual-circuit braking systems, complete brake failure is very rare, but it can still occur. If the cause is a slow leak of hydraulic fluid, you may have some warning from the pedal, which will travel further and may feel 'spongy'. Pumping hard to bring more fluid into the system can produce a temporary improvement, but the cause must be rectified before you lose the brakes altogether.

Sooner or later you will experience reduced braking performance in wet weather. Prolonged driving in rain can cause a film of water to build up between brake disc and pad, with the result that the brakes cannot work efficiently. It is wise, therefore, to apply the brakes occasionally to keep them free of water, but only when no vehicles are close behind.

In the event of complete brake failure, you must do your best with handbrake and gearbox, dropping down through the gears as briskly as possible in order to maximise engine braking.

Using the handbrake

Except in an emergency, the handbrake should only be used when your car is stationary. Learner drivers are taught to pull on the handbrake every time they stop, but in many circumstances this is quite unnecessary. You will tend to apply the handbrake at traffic lights, but not necessarily when stopping briefly at a 'stop' sign.

If you come to rest on a hill, of course, using the handbrake is essential. Holding your car on a gradient by slipping the clutch wears it out unnecessarily quickly.

Protect the ratchet mechanism by pressing the release button whenever you apply the handbrake.

Allowing for other drivers

Keep a very close eye on your mirrors in dense traffic, and give early warning of your braking to drivers following too closely.

Before braking, always keep a watchful eye on the drivers around you. Be prepared for the driver in front to pull up sharply without any obvious reason. Look out, too, for someone in a crumpled old banger looming up in your mirrors, and allow for the fact that its brakes might not be as good as those on your car.

Make allowances for the irritating driver who 'rides' your back bumper. Try to give extra warning by braking earlier than usual, starting with a light touch on the pedal to bring on your brake lights. Leave yourself more space than normal so that your gentle braking gives the thoughtless driver behind more stopping distance.

With any 'tailgating' driver, avoid the temptation to 'teach a lesson' by banging on your brakes, since this could put both of you in danger. It is better to slow right down and encourage such a driver to pass, or you can even consider pulling in to a lay-by to get rid of a menace.

Advanced checklist

- Brake smoothly and progressively. Ease onto the pedal when you start braking, increase the pressure through the middle phase of braking, then release the pedal gradually towards the end of your braking.
- Always be aware of the braking distance you need at any speed, and allow for thinking distance too in the gap you leave behind the vehicle in front.
- Always try to brake in a straight line because sudden braking in a corner can unsettle your car.
- Always test your brakes before starting out on a journey and choose a safe moment to check them again.
- Familiarise yourself with your car's braking ability, and try to practise cadence braking to avoid locking the wheels in an emergency.
- Allow for other drivers around you in the use of your brakes.

What the examiner looks for

- Is your braking smooth and progressive, or late and fierce?
- Are the brakes used in conjunction with mirror and signals?
- Are road, traffic and weather conditions taken into account?
- Do you ever show bad planning by braking in two or more phases on the approach to a hazard?
- Do you try to avoid overlapping your braking with gearchanges or steering?
- Do you use the handbrake correctly?

Driving for economy

The way you drive

The good anticipation involved in advanced driving provides a welcome bonus at the filling station.

Advanced driving in many ways goes hand in hand with economical driving. Avoiding unnecessary revving of the engine, applying good acceleration sense, braking gently in good time and using the gears correctly all contribute to improving your fuel consumption and minimising expensive wear and tear on your car.

The advanced driver seeks a happy balance between making good progress and driving economically. There are many ways you can do this. Accelerating briskly to a cruising speed means that you spend a greater proportion of a given journey in top gear. Using a good anticipation to avoid unnecessary braking always saves fuel. Driving at a constant cruising speed with a feathered throttle is more economical than the slight fluctuations in speed that many inattentive drivers unknowingly use on the open road.

Moving along in stop-start traffic gives you plenty of opportunities to save fuel. Pull away from rest with minimal revs and take your foot off the accelerator as soon as you see traffic ahead stopping again, so that engine braking is your main means of slowing down. In sluggish traffic you can sometimes open up a gap behind a vehicle that allows you to move forwards at a more or less constant trickle, despite drivers ahead stopping and starting far more frequently. In prolonged hold-ups you will consider switching off your engine until you see traffic ahead starting to move again.

Labouring your engine normally means that you use more fuel than necessary. Many drivers hold on to a high gear for too long going up a hill, changing down only when the engine struggles. With good anticipation, you can sometimes accelerate when you see a hill ahead so that you can ascend it in a higher gear without asking too much from your engine. This forward planning can improve your progress and save fuel.

Diesel versus petrol

The decision to buy a diesel rather than a petrol car on the grounds of economy is not as clear-cut as it may seem. Generally a diesel costs more to buy than its petrol-engined equivalent, new or secondhand, so the fuel savings only become worthwhile if you cover a fairly high mileage.

A small-engined car is not necessarily the most economical, especially if your driving involves plenty of long journeys at higher speeds. A car of similar size but with a larger engine and taller gearing can be more economical because it does not have to work as hard.

Safety before economy

Never put fuel economy before safety. Forget about economical driving when you need swift acceleration or a burst of speed. Never coast down a hill to save a bit of fuel. Remember, too, that an advanced driver seeks to make good progress.

Persistently driving in top gear at the lowest possible speed, irrespective of the road and traffic conditions, irritates everyone who is delayed and can cause danger if drivers behind become frustrated. The mean-minded or over-cautious driver at the front of the queue plays a part in the danger when an impatient driver overtakes recklessly.

Advanced checklist

- The principles of advanced driving generally help fuel economy, but think about how you can improve economy still further.
- Avoiding putting economy before safety and driving slowly enough to be a nuisance to other road users.
- Think about fuel economy when you choose your car. What size of engine? Petrol or diesel?

What the examiner looks for

- Do you drive with a reasonable sense of economy, avoiding excessive revs and unnecessary braking?
- Do you hang on to low gears for too long or labour the engine in the higher gears?
- Is your anticipation good enough to produce a dividend in economical driving?
- Do you strike the right balance between making good progress and driving economically?

Sympathy and understanding

Mechanical sympathy

A significant benefit of advanced driving techniques is that they go hand in hand with mechanical sympathy. Helped by knowledge of their cars and respect for them, advanced drivers avoid clumsy or violent use of the controls, thereby minimising wear and tear on all mechanical parts. When conditions are right they use performance to the full, but never abuse it.

'Racing' starts at traffic lights use more fuel and give the transmission a hard time. Late and excessive braking shortens the life of pads or shoes and wears out the tyres more quickly. Clumsy gearchanging wears out the gearbox and clutch. Coarse steering and excessive cornering speeds shorten tyre and suspension life. Driving too fast over bumpy roads or traffic-calming measures brings forward the day when shock absorbers have to be renewed.

The engine can be abused as well. By all means use its performance when it is safe to do so, but letting the revs soar habitually to the limit will wear it out more quickly. Likewise you can labour an engine by asking it to pull hard at low revs in a high gear. Advanced drivers develop an instinctive feeling for a car's performance and make sure they are always in the right gear for the conditions.

Looking after your tyres

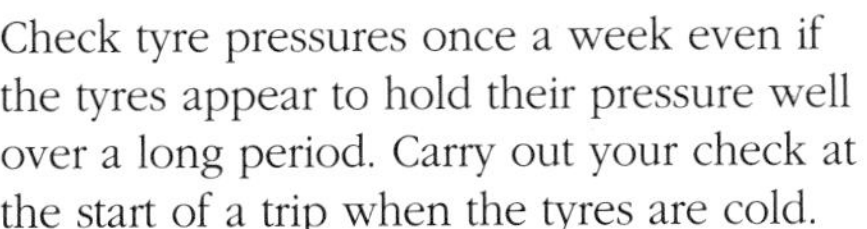

These worn-out tyres show the effects of under-inflation (top), over-inflation (centre) and misaligned tracking (bottom).

Check tyre pressures once a week even if the tyres appear to hold their pressure well over a long period. Carry out your check at the start of a trip when the tyres are cold.

Follow the manufacturer's recommended pressures, using common sense to make slight variations – perhaps by adding a few pounds when carrying a heavy load – if you feel they are necessary. At the same time prise any small stones out of the treads and check the sidewalls for cuts or bulges.

Under-inflation causes serious problems when cornering because the sidewalls can move sideways relative to the wheel rim. This significantly reduces grip and can make your car feel unpredictable. Under-inflation also causes heat to build up in a tyre, increasing the rate of wear and leading in extreme circumstances to chunks of tread breaking off the carcass. Soft tyres are easily damaged and increase fuel consumption.

Over-inflation results in the tyre bulging in the centre of the tread pattern so that only a small section is in contact with the road. As much as half of the grip can be lost, and the central part of the tread will wear rapidly.

The law requires that a tyre must be replaced when tread depth has worn down to 1.6mm. This is lenient. A tyre's grip in wet weather will have deteriorated considerably by this point, so it is wise to consider renewal before tread depth reaches 3mm.

Careless driving can damage your car's tyres and compromise safety. Mounting a kerb, dropping a wheel into a deep pothole or scraping a tyre against a kerb can rupture a sidewall.

Although it is known that one accident in six on motorways results from tyre failure, most drivers pay far too little attention to the condition of their tyres.

Avoiding clutch abuse

A clutch can last for 100,000 miles if treated with respect, yet a driver with no mechanical sympathy can ruin one within 5000 miles.

A driver who uses the clutch pedal as a rest for the left foot can cause the clutch to slip a little all the time. Instead of using the handbrake correctly, a lazy driver resorts to the clutch to hold the car on a hill, balancing the biting point against engine revs so that the car remains stationary. Slipping the clutch occurs when it is released too gently or too sharply after a gearchange. Using excessive revs when moving away from rest or applying power too early after a gearchange also damages the clutch.

Advanced checklist

- Drive with mechanical sympathy: avoid using the brakes too harshly and do not extend the engine above or below its comfortable operating range.
- Treating the clutch with respect is an area where the advanced driver really stands out from the pack.
- Keep a regular eye on tyre condition by checking pressures and making sure no damage has occurred.
- A car is extremely dangerous on worn tyres in all conditions, but especially in wet weather.

What the examiner looks for

- Does your car appear to be well maintained?
- Are its tyres in good condition and properly inflated?
- Do you abuse your car, perhaps by revving the engine needlessly or braking too fiercely?
- Is the clutch treated properly when changing gear or moving away from standstill?

3 APPLYING ADVANCED DRIVING METHODS

Junctions

The special care needed at junctions

Any junction requires extra alertness and concentration, especially when traffic is heavy. This is Trafalgar Square in London.

You face extra risks wherever roads meet, whether at crossroads, T-junctions, side turnings, roundabouts or forks. Most accidents occur when vehicles come into conflict with each other, something that happens mainly at junctions.

Accidents do not 'just happen'. In 95 per cent of cases they are caused by the mistakes made by all road users. Be on your guard, therefore, for 'accidents waiting to happen'. By using the techniques of advanced driving and applying a systematic approach, however, junctions can be dealt with as safely as any other part of the road system.

Crossroads and T-junctions

When you are approaching on the minor route, or when neither route has precedence, pay careful attention to your speed and position on the road. Take up the correct position and begin braking at an early stage after checking mirrors and signalling if necessary. If there is a 'stop' sign you will actually come to a halt, using the handbrake if traffic means a stop of more than a few seconds.

If there are no lane markings, position yourself positively as you approach and arrive at the junction. If turning left, you should be close to the nearside. If you turning right, you should be close to the centre line. If at a crossroads and planning to go straight ahead, you should aim to take up an informative position, which may be somewhere in the middle, but you will avoid being an obstacle to drivers behind who want to go in a different direction. If a vehicle is waiting at the road opposite, be certain of the driver's intentions before you move away.

Keep your patience under control when traffic is heavy. A gap may look big enough for you to slip into it if you accelerate hard enough, but resist the temptation to cut the margins too fine. The

A common scenario: it cannot be assumed that the approaching car will turn into the side road. The driver may have left the indicators flashing by mistake or may be planning to park just after the junction.

approaching driver may be slow to react and your actions should not cause someone to brake.

While you wait for a break in the traffic, always be aware of a common cause of accidents. A vehicle approaching from your right and signalling left appears to be telling you that it will turn into your road, allowing you to move away. But indicators can be left on by mistake, or the driver, unaware that a confusing message is being given, may be planning to pull in immediately after passing your junction.

Good positioning when turning left or right at a T-junction or crossroads.

Never assume that the vehicle will turn until you actually see the driver begin moving into another road. The only reliable information obtained from a flashing indicator is that the bulb is working.

Using the more major of the two routes at a crossroads or junction does not entitle you to drive as you like. A driver may still make an unsignalled, sudden turn in front of you or may slow down abruptly. Someone waiting to pull out from a side road may do so in front of you. When approaching a vehicle waiting to turn into your road, observe the driver and be very cautious if you think you have not been seen.

In any instances where you think another vehicle may move into your path without warning, consider 'covering' the brake pedal – holding your right foot poised above it – so that you can react more quickly.

Show consideration to other road users, but not so excessively that you put politeness before practicality. By all means let someone out of a side turning if it is safe to do so, but it is foolish if you have to cause drivers behind you to brake. Misplaced courtesy can cause problems for other road users who are not expecting it.

Turning right at crossroads

Right turns at crossroads can be more complicated because of the confusion which arises with opposing traffic also waiting to turn right. Where there are no road markings, half of the country's drivers seem to favour passing offside-to-offside, the other half nearside-to-nearside. The *Highway Code* makes the preferred approach perfectly clear.

Aim to pass offside-to-offside. In other words, pass behind an opposing vehicle waiting to turn right. Do

otherwise only when road markings, junction layout or the position of other vehicles dictate it. Passing round behind other traffic gives you a clear view ahead as you make your turn, whereas the nearside-to-nearside approach can force you to nose out blindly across the traffic stream. It is hardly surprising that so many accidents occur where traffic turns right.

Two drivers turning right at a crossroads should aim to pass each other offside-to-offside. With nearside-to-nearside passing (top diagram), the view of oncoming traffic is obscured.

Traffic lights

When you come to a stop, secure your car on the handbrake and then move the gear lever to neutral.

If you can see the lights controlling routes crossing your path, keep an eye on them so that you have advance warning of when your lights are about to change. Traffic movement gives you the same message if you watch for the first sign of a vehicle stopping. You can use this observation to select first gear a few seconds before you expect to move away, but not to take liberties with the lights by moving at 'red and amber'.

Advanced observation approaching traffic lights can help you make better progress. If you have a choice of lanes, take the 'lane of least resistance' – the one with less traffic in it. Poor lane discipline on urban dual-carriageways often means that the nearside lane is emptier. In a right-hand lane, pick up at an early stage road markings which indicate that it can be shared by traffic going straight ahead and turning right. Good observation prevents you being delayed behind right-turn traffic when you want to go straight on.

Observing the lane pattern beyond the lights may influence your position. Where three lanes go down to two, or two down to one, you will judge which approach lane will allow you to make the best and safest progress after the lights.

Since there is often insufficient warning of filter lights ahead, sooner or later on an unfamiliar road you will find yourself in the wrong lane, perhaps coming up to a green left-turn filter when you wish to go straight on. Do not attempt to find a way into the correct traffic stream if this means forcing a gap for yourself or delaying vehicles behind you. You must make the turn indicated by the filter and retrace your route.

There is an increasing tendency for drivers of all vehicles to cross red lights. An automatic camera sequence taken on a London dual-carriageway shows *seven* vehicles, four of them trucks, driving through *six* seconds after the lights turned red. This use of cameras is likely to become a growing deterrent, but drive with discretion even when the lights are green.

Sooner or later on unfamiliar roads you will find yourself in the wrong lane on the approach to filter lights. Rather than try to push your way into the traffic flow in the lane you want, keep to your wrong course and turn round at the first safe opportunity.

Roundabouts

Positioning and signalling are very important at roundabouts, and you should strike the right balance between reserve and haste by making a decisive, safe entry into the traffic flow.

During the approach to a roundabout, the experienced driver gauges the speed and pattern of traffic already on the roundabout. Sometimes it is possible to time your arrival perfectly, at the moment when a gap appears – and often you will make better progress than the traffic around you. When traffic is light enough, it should be possible to enter a roundabout where the view is good with only a modest reduction in speed. But judge this carefully and always allow for another driver taking a similarly decisive approach at the previous entry.

If traffic is heavy you will simply have to wait at the entry road for a suitable gap. Many drivers are clueless about positioning and signalling on roundabouts, so do not assume that vehicles on the roundabout will do as you expect.

Priority is sometimes given to a major route passing through a roundabout. For a driver in an unfamiliar area, the need to give way while on the roundabout can cause a moment's confusion, but the advanced driver's observation skills always pick up this situation well ahead.

Mini roundabouts

You should aim to take the defined course through a mini roundabout, but some are so tight that it is difficult to avoid putting a wheel on the centre circle.

Mini roundabouts are used to control traffic where there is no room for a more conventional layout, or to give priority to intersecting roads without the need for traffic lights, usually because traffic is light most of the day or a particular junction has a bad accident record.

Some mini roundabouts can cause problems. When you encounter a cluster of two or three of them you need a very high level of observation: keep an eye on traffic on all sides and watch out for unexpected movements from confused or indecisive drivers. The reduced traffic separation at the most compact mini roundabouts also requires extra care.

Although you will always try to take the defined course through a mini roundabout, some are so tight or badly designed that it is difficult to avoid putting a wheel on the centre circle.

Signalling on roundabouts

Good signalling and positioning at roundabouts keep others informed of your intentions. Use of the indicators is so often neglected, as with the red car and the lorry here.

On all normal roundabouts you should keep to the established procedure outlined in the *Highway Code* unless lane markings tell you to do differently.

If you plan to take the first exit, move into the left-hand lane and signal a left turn on your approach, keeping your indicators going until your chosen exit point is reached.

If you plan to go more or less straight across, it is preferable to keep to the left on your approach and through the roundabout, signalling a left turn after passing the exit before the one you intend to take. Good observation will bring you into the left lane in good time as you approach the roundabout, but if traffic is slow-moving you might be able to make better progress in the right-hand lane.

Once you are on the roundabout, a course in the right-hand lane demands impeccable mirror work, and maybe even a glance over your left shoulder, before you commit yourself to your exit. A wrongly-positioned driver to your nearside may be intending to take the next exit.

When choosing an exit more than 180 degrees round, you will stay in the right-hand lane, signalling a right turn in plenty of time. Again you must allow for the driver who has come with you on your nearside and wants the exit after the one you have chosen, so use your mirrors well.

Advanced checklist

- Remember that all junctions create extra danger: always signal your intentions well in advance, take up the correct position on the road and move off only when you are certain it is safe to do so.
- When turning right at a crossroads, pass oncoming vehicles also turning right offside-to-offside, unless road markings, junction layout or the position of other vehicles dictate otherwise.
- Always use the correct lane and signalling procedure when approaching and negotiating roundabouts; your entry to a roundabout should be carefully-judged, decisive and safe.
- Never assume that a vehicle will follow the path suggested by its indicators.
- If you expect to be stopped at a junction for more than a few seconds, secure your car on the handbrake and put the gear lever in neutral.

What the examiner looks for

- Are signals, signs and road markings observed, obeyed and approached correctly?
- Is the correct road position taken up at an early stage during the approach to a junction?
- When you arrive at a 'stop' sign, do you actually come to a halt and consider applying the handbrake?
- Are roundabouts negotiated safely, with a well-timed approach, correct signalling, good positioning and a confident entry?

Giving signals

The art of good signalling

Giving the correct signals at the right time and in the right way is an essential part of advanced driving. Visible and audible signals are your main means of communication to warn others of your intentions and presence.

Signals are used to inform other road users, not to give orders to them. A signal never gives you the right to make a move, such as a lane change on a dual-carriageway or motorway, on the assumption that others will give way.

Do not expect other road users to react in the right way to your correct signalling. Another driver may not see your signal, or interpret it correctly, or act on it sensibly. Since you can never be certain that others will recognise your intentions, always drive so that you can change your plans if your signals are ignored.

Direction indicators

Most of the signals you make while driving involve direction indicators. They are used not only when turning left and right, but also before changing your position on the road. Use them thoughtfully and in good time so that other road users know what you are doing and can take action accordingly.

Bring good judgement to your use of the indicators. Late signalling or the failure to give a signal at all are among the most common faults you see in day-to-day driving.

Late signalling or the failure to give a signal at all are among the most common faults you see in day-to-day driving. As an advanced driver make sure you are never guilty of this – but remember that signalling too early can also be misleading.

Avoid thinking that a signal is unnecessary at quiet times of day or night just because few people are about. But indicators can also be used over-zealously.

When driving along an urban road dotted with parked cars, there is no need to signal every time you prepare to pass one. It is unnecessary to signal out of habit at country lane junctions if you really are on your own. Signalling left when you finish overtaking on a motorway is only useful if it benefits other drivers, such as someone in the left-hand lane who may be about to move into the middle lane at the same time as you head for it from the right-hand lane.

Never use one signal to cover two manoeuvres. For example, if you intend to turn left at a junction and then park on the left immediately afterwards, you could confuse a driver behind if you keep the left indicator flashing without a break. In this situation your intentions can be conveyed in various ways: you may have time to interrupt your signal to make the point; you will consider a hand signal before pulling in at the left; you may be able to communicate your plans by adjusting your road position.

In some circumstances self-cancelling stops your indicators when you still need them. Turning right at a roundabout is a common example: having to steer left at the entry to a roundabout often cancels your right-turn signal. With lane changes, of course, you have to cancel the indicators yourself, but so many people forget.

Hand signals

There are occasions when the advanced driver should consider using the two basic hand signals – extending your arm to indicate a right turn or rotating it anti-clockwise to indicate a left turn. A hand signal is advisable when you are not certain that your direction indicator has been seen (such as in bright sunlight) or when you feel that emphasis of your intentions would be helpful.

A likely instance occurs when you plan to turn right where two side roads are close to each other, and you want to make it clear which one you are going to take. A right-turn hand signal can also be valuable to emphasise that you are intending to turn right and are not just pulling out to pass a parked vehicle.

In heavy or fast-moving traffic, a left-turn hand signal can usefully confirm an intention to pull in at the side of the road or take a small side turning if you think your maneouvre might surprise a driver behind.

Remember also that these hand signals – as well as the upright palm signal indicating an intention to go straight ahead – can be useful in communicating your plans to a police officer controlling traffic at a junction.

Although you do not often see it used, the 'I intend to slow down' signal – an up-and-down movement of the right arm with the palm facing downwards – can be useful to emphasise the intentions shown by your brake lights. The right time for this signal is when you think a driver behind is too close or driving inattentively, and therefore might not realise that you are coming to a halt in traffic. The signal is particularly appropriate when you stop at a pedestrian crossing, since it warns drivers not to overtake as you slow down.

Brake lights

Your brake lights cannot be misunderstood by anybody: they work automatically and the message is totally clear. The advanced driver, however, can use brake lights thoughtfully to convey additional information to drivers behind.

If you consider that a car is following too closely, it is a good idea when you approach a hazard to brake lightly at first to give the driver time to drop back to a safe distance before you have to brake more firmly. Leave extra stopping distance to give yourself room to do this.

Thoughtful communication with your brake lights can be useful if your car is the last in a queue of traffic stopped unexpectedly, perhaps just over the brow of a hill, round a bend or on a fast road. When you see a vehicle in your mirrors, applying the brakes at intervals, even when stationary, will warn the driver that little bit earlier that traffic is at a standstill and not just moving slowly.

The horn

You may not use the horn often, but to believe that it should never be used is a mistake.

The horn should be sounded only if you need to warn other road users of your presence. It should be used sparingly, but you should not be reluctant to use it firmly at the right time as it can be a life-saver. It is illegal, except in an emergency to avoid an accident, to sound your horn between 11.30pm and 7.00am in a built-up area, or if your car is stationary.

There are three situations when using the horn should be considered. First, it can serve as warning of your approach when the view ahead is very limited, perhaps before a blind bend on a narrow lane or when nearing a dangerous crossroads where the side roads are obscured by hedges.

Second, the horn can be valuable when another road user is vulnerable despite your safety precautions – children, cyclists and pedestrians might benefit.

Third, a firm but polite note on the horn can be used when you are about to overtake another vehicle whose driver may not have noticed you – this is often appropriate when passing a large truck or tractor.

Do not assume that your horn will have been heard. The person you are aiming it at may be deaf or may have the car radio turned up loud.

Never use the horn as a substitute for the observation, planning and courtesy which are the mark of a good driver. Remember that British drivers seem far more ready than their continental counterparts to take offence at the sound of a horn, so use it with discretion. If they think that a note on the horn is not delivered politely, some drivers take it as a reprimand, a challenge or an insult, and react accordingly.

Thoughtful and courteous use of the horn is what counts. You may not use it often, but to believe that it should never be used is a mistake.

Headlight flashing

Headlight flashes should be used only for one purpose: to inform other road users that you are there. Headlight flashes are useful when the horn would not be heard and in place of the horn at night. Use good judgement to decide the timing and duration of the flash.

Any other use of headlight flashing gives rise to confusion because your message might be interpreted as meaning something quite different. Attempting to give an order ('get out of my way'), offer an invitation ('you may come through this gap I have left'), issue a rebuke ('your bad driving has just caused me to brake') or make an acknowledgement ('thank you for waiting') can be misunderstood. Never assume that it is safe to proceed as a result of a flash from another motorist – this is well-meaning but the driver may have made an error of judgement.

Before overtaking, a headlight flash can be helpful if you think the other driver is unaware of your intention. Headlight flashing at night can usefully emphasise your presence. Consider it on the approach to a hump-back bridge, a blind bend or a sharp crest on a narrow road. But do not give these signals if they might be misunderstood by road users for whom they are not intended.

Truck drivers have their own headlight code, whereby one driver tells another overtaking driver when it is safe to pull back to the nearside. As a car driver there is no need for you to adopt this practice: imagine the distracting light show that would occur on motorways and dual-carriageways if everyone did it.

Hazard warning lights

These are used to alert other drivers to your presence when you have stopped in a dangerous place. As well as switching them on if your car breaks down or is involved in an accident, you should consider using them when you stop at the tail of an unexpected queue.

The only occasion when hazard warning lights should be used while your car is moving is to give extra warning to vehicles behind when you encounter a hold-up on a motorway or dual-carriageway.

Hazard warning lights should not be used as an excuse for parking illegally or in an unsafe place.

Hazard warning lights can cause confusion. This van appears to be about to pull out, but sharp observation spots the left-hand indicator visible through the car's windows.

Courtesy signals

Signalling to say 'thank you' when someone leaves a gap for you or lets you go first can do a great deal to improve road safety in general. All road users like to be thanked for courteous and considerate driving, and showing your appreciation with a wave – or just by opening your palm from the steering wheel – will encourage someone to co-operate again. In a situation where it seems unwise to take one hand off the steering wheel, a nod of the head and a smile will convey the same message.

You should also use a wave to apologise for a mistake in your driving. If you inadvertently 'carve up' another driver, an angry or aggressive reaction is far less likely if you acknowledge your error.

Misplaced courtesy

Some drivers wrongly use two hand signals in the belief that they are being courteous to other road users. These are the 'You can overtake me' wave to a following vehicle and the 'Please cross' gesture to pedestrians.

The problem with these is that if you make a mistake you could be guilty of causing an accident through your good intentions. It is not always possible for you to judge whether other road users – drivers or pedestrians – can safely accept your invitation. Leave it to them to make their own judgement.

Since irresponsible drivers seem increasingly willing to break the law by overtaking on either side of traffic halted at a pedestrian crossing, the consequences of someone stepping into the road at your request could be serious.

Never invite pedestrians to cross the road – they could be exposed to danger that you have not spotted.

Advanced checklist

- Use your direction indicators to inform other road users of your intentions, not to give orders to them. Use them correctly, consistently and thoughtfully.
- Remember that headlight flashes can be misunderstood by other road users: flash your headlights only when it is useful to warn others of your presence and when your intentions cannot be misinterpreted.
- Use the horn in the same way as headlight flashes – to let other road users know you are there.
- If safe to do so, give a courtesy wave when you benefit from considerate behaviour.
- Apart from the courtesy gesture of acknowledgement, use only the hand signals given in the *Highway Code;* these should be used in circumstances where road users would benefit from emphasis of your intentions.

What the examiner looks for

- Are direction indicator signals – and hand signals when needed – given at the right place and in good time?
- Are the horn and headlight flasher used in accordance with the *Highway Code*?

Cornering

The pleasures of cornering

Cornering with precision, confidence and safety on a country road – real driving for pleasure.

The most enjoyable driving you ever do comes on quiet country roads with all their variety of interesting corners, open views of the road, gentle ups and downs and pleasant scenery. Cornering your car with precision, at a confident but safe speed, is part of the pleasure.

All driving requires first-class concentration and observation. If you fail to apply these disciplines when driving through corners, sooner or later you will be caught by surprise – maybe a bend tightens up, you brake too late or the surface deteriorates. Your car's reserves of grip and handling will probably keep you on the road, but you will feel uncomfortable, even shaken. In putting speed before safety, you will not have behaved like an advanced driver.

Cornering procedure

Generalisations are limited because every corner is different, but this should be your basic procedure:

- As the corner approaches, check your mirrors in case someone is coming up fast and possibly contemplating an overtaking manoeuvre when the view ahead is limited.
- Judge the appropriate speed and road position for the corner and carry out any necessary braking while your car is still travelling in a straight line. Your speed through the corner should allow you to stop within the distance you can see to be clear.
- When you finish braking, change to a lower gear if necessary. Your gearchange should be made before you turn into the corner.
- Observe the road surface for any irregularities – such as a drain at the lowest point of the camber – that may influence your choice of line.
- Start steering into the corner, using a progressive movement. Abrupt steering will put more load on the tyres and cause your car to roll more.
- Press the accelerator slightly as the car responds to the steering. Any car will feel a little steadier under gentle power, but your aim is only to maintain speed, not to accelerate.
- Keep looking towards the limit of your vision to check that the road is clear. Your speed will allow you to stop within the distance you can see, and careful positioning can improve your view.
- When your view opens up and you start to straighten the steering, push the accelerator a little more firmly to build up speed again. Acceleration should be tailored to road conditions and should remain gentle until the road is straight. Early or excessive acceleration could cause your car to run wide.

Cornering forces

Drivers rarely have anyone to blame but themselves if they go off the road on a bend. The results are especially disastrous if such foolhardy driving results in a collision with another vehicle.

Excuses may be given about adverse camber, the road being greasy or the bend tightening up unexpectedly. Any of these can be factors in an accident, but not the cause. Unless mechanical or tyre failure occurs, the reason is bad driving.

It may be helpful to consider how cornering forces affect the behaviour of a car through a bend. When driving round a bend the force required to do this is applied by the action of the road on the front tyres. You feel as if you are being pushed out towards the side of the car, an illusion arising from the fact that you only turn into the bend when the car pushes against you.

If the friction force of the road on the tyres is insufficient, you will skid as the car tries to continue along its straight-line path. This can arise from excessive speed, bald tyres, wet leaves or slippery surfaces.

Positioning for the best view

Careful adjustment of road position improves the view through a corner.

The best course through a corner means adjusting your position on the road to seek two benefits – to obtain the best view ahead and to 'straighten' the curve. Considerations of safety, road surface, other road users and visibility all affect your decision about how much of the width of your carriageway you use when negotiating a bend.

For left-hand bends, you obtain the best view by taking up a position towards the centre of the road. You should hold this position through the bend until the view opens up, then sweep smoothly towards the nearside to straighten the last part of the corner. Flattening the curve once you have a good view reduces the cornering force acting on your car and allows you to start accelerating at an earlier stage.

When visibility is limited, a positive, but safe, position towards the crown of the road allows an oncoming car to be seen slightly sooner.

For right-hand bends, maximising your view means that you approach on the nearside, and then choose a gradual curve towards the centre as soon as you can see through the corner. Again this straightening of the last part of the curve improves grip and allows earlier acceleration, as well as reducing the effect of the adverse camber that must be expected on a right-hander.

The moment when you can start to straighten a corner will occur sooner on an open bend than on one bounded by tall hedges or walls. Another advantage of good positioning is that it puts you on a 'late entry, early exit' course, which avoids the common error of drifting dangerously wide – and towards oncoming traffic in a left-hander – through the last part of a corner.

Adjustments of position must be made with such subtlety and discretion that they never alarm other drivers or reduce your margin for error. Their purpose is improved safety, not higher cornering speeds. Generally you will minimise position changes when facing oncoming vehicles.

Exaggerated positioning is definitely to be discouraged. Avoid going too close to the verge and tick yourself off if you feel your offside wheels touching the central cat's eyes.

Observing the road surface

Alarming moments can occur during cornering because a driver fails to slow down enough to cope comfortably with a poor road surface. Normal common sense will tell you to reduce cornering speeds in wet or freezing conditions, but an extra edge of observation will pick up mud or gravel, a sunken drain (often found at the apex of a corner), wet leaves, severe bumps and potholes.

Minor roads often have pronounced camber, which can influence your position and speed through a bend. Camber is the convex surface profile that allows water to drain towards either side of the road. This slope generally assists you through a left-hander and acts against you through a right-hander, but there are always exceptions.

Modern roads have a 'super-elevated' profile, which removes the surprises that camber changes can bring. Super-elevation banks up the whole width of the road towards the outside edge of the bend, making the slope favourable for cornering in both directions.

Braking in a corner

It is important to complete your braking before turning into a corner. Braking in a bend (see page 32) upsets your car's balance and loads up the outside front tyre. In extreme circumstances, heavy braking on a slippery surface could cause you to lose control.

Twisty country roads keep you on your toes. A compact sequence of S-bends with a tight one at the end, for example, requires precision in finding a brief period of straight-line travel for braking. Even if the car never actually travels in a straight line, there is always an ideal moment between left-hand and right-hand lock when you can brake without unsettling the car.

Every now and then an exceptionally tricky corner – perhaps a long, tightening, downhill one – may prevent you from obeying the rule, but observation should be good enough for any use of the brakes to be merely gentle and precautionary.

An unexpected hazard, such as a broken-down car, makes braking on a bend unavoidable. Try to apply the brakes progressively and steer into any skid (see page 58).

Forward planning normally avoids braking in a bend, which can unsettle the car – especially if there is a sharp crest as well.

Advanced checklist

- Aim to complete your braking and any change to a lower gear before you turn the steering.
- Always take a corner at a speed that allows you to stop within the distance you can see to be clear.
- When road and traffic conditions permit, position your car for the best view through a corner, using the methods described for left-handers and right-handers.
- Corners are best taken smoothly at a constant speed or with moderate acceleration once the exit line is clear.
- You must avoid excessive braking or acceleration on bends unless an emergency leaves you no alternative.

What the examiner looks for

- Are bends and corners taken safely and at a suitable speed?
- Do you demonstrate good positioning when approaching, negotiating and leaving a corner?
- Is your steering smooth and progressive?
- Does poor planning ever cause you to brake in a bend?
- Do you take account of road surface irregularities when choosing your line and speed through a corner?

Overtaking

Do you need to overtake?

Always question whether you have anything to gain by overtaking on a two-way road. It is normally worth planning to overtake one or two vehicles that are significantly restricting your progress along a relatively quiet road. Often, however, overtaking is pointless if it serves only to move you one place up a queue.

Think about those occasions when you travel in a long row of vehicles and one impatient driver tries to pick them off one after another, darting in and out for mile after mile, sitting on back bumpers, alarming oncoming drivers, bullying a path into inadequate gaps and forcing other drivers to brake. The level of danger is raised for everyone, but all this driver achieves is to jump a few places forward. Sometimes all this reckless work is undone when this character inevitably chooses the right-hand lane at a queue into a roundabout, only to find one of those 'victims' moving unobtrusively past in the left-hand lane.

In advanced driving, good observation and thinking always avoids unnecessary overtaking. Do not search fruitlessly for an overtaking opportunity if conditions are likely to change within a mile or two. You may know from familiarity or route planning that a dual-carriageway is not far away. Sometimes you can reasonably expect a slow-moving vehicle – perhaps a tractor, postal van or delivery van – to stop or turn off quite soon. If a town is approaching, some of the vehicles delaying you are likely to disperse and you may be able to pass others by choosing a favourable lane at a junction. Many factors such as these should be considered.

Judging when to overtake

That clear stretch of road offers a tempting overtaking opportunity, but the manoeuvre must be delayed. The car in the side turning is waiting to turn towards you. Its driver, seeing no vehicles to the right, could move off without looking in your direction.

Overtaking requires careful planning, rapid thinking and decisiveness. You must be certain that the road is clear far enough ahead to avoid alarming an oncoming driver or forcing the driver you are passing to take action to help you out of a sticky situation. You must have good judgement of your car's acceleration abilities and its response in the appropriate gear.

You should never overtake when approaching a side turning, even if there is no-one waiting to pull out. As well as signposted junctions, driveways, laybys and even field entrances must also be observed.

Junctions to the right are particularly dangerous: the vehicle you plan to overtake could turn right without warning, or a vehicle could emerge from the junction. One scenario happens all too often: a driver pauses to join a main road, looks to the right to check that nothing is coming, and then pulls out without thinking that an overtaking car could be approaching from the left.

Before overtaking, make sure you have an empty stretch of road to return to. A lorry can hide a slow-moving car ahead of it, so vary your position on the road and use views through corners to confirm that space is available. Poor observation is the only reason for a driver suddenly finding that two vehicles must be passed instead of one. You also need to be aware of traffic that may be slowing down ahead.

Always be prepared to flash your headlights or sound your horn to draw attention to yourself. Normally the need for this occurs if you think the driver you are overtaking may be unaware of your presence. As well as alerting inattentive car drivers, this warning can be useful when you prepare to pass tractors, heavy lorries or caravans.

Make use of your local knowledge but do not put implicit trust in it. Consider this example: you know the tractor that holds you up most mornings always turns left into the same gateway without signalling, but one day it might turn right without signalling.

Overtaking must be planned with great care, not with the air of optimism that a few irresponsible drivers employ. There is a simple guiding rule: if in doubt hold back.

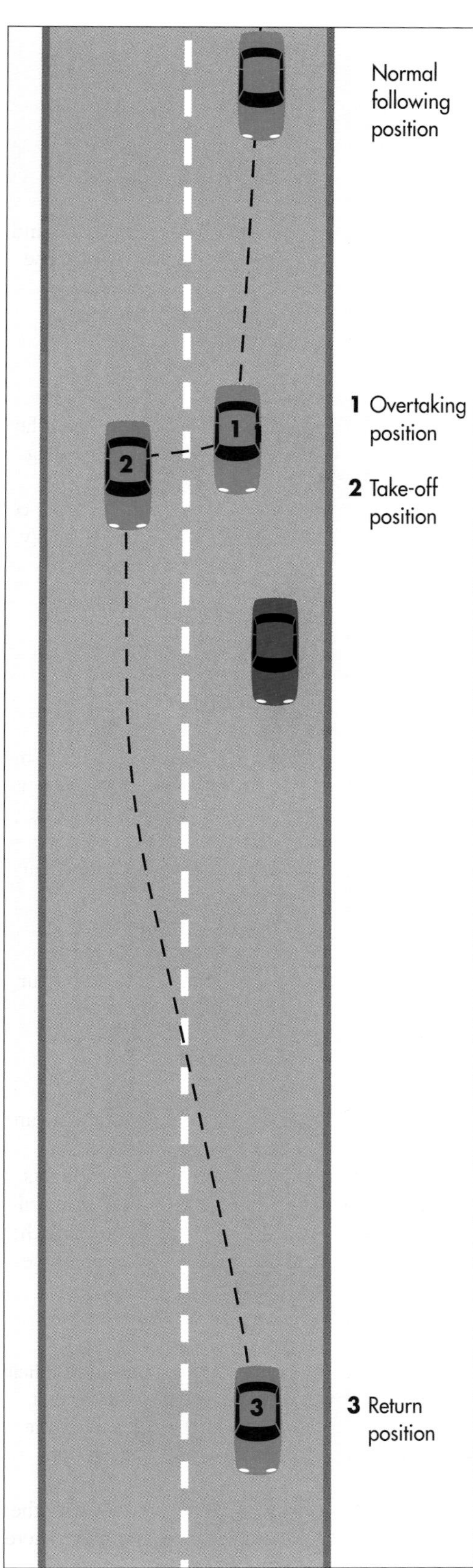

The overtaking triangle

Police drivers are taught a three-point overtaking pattern which defines the correct position for your car through the manoeuvre. It is the safest, quickest and most efficient way of overtaking, but skilful use of it is rarely seen on public roads.

The overtaking position
This is the first 'corner' of the overtaking triangle. Consider selecting a lower gear when your long-range observation tells you that a possible overtaking opportunity is a few seconds away, then gradually close in on the vehicle in front to take up the overtaking position. This means sacrificing your safe following distance temporarily, but not excessively. You also move towards the centre line to maximise your view. If the expected opportunity does not arise, slip back to your safe following distance and consider returning to a higher gear while you wait for another chance.

The take-off position
This is the second 'corner' of the overtaking triangle. When an overtaking opportunity arrives, move smoothly out to a position of maximum visibility, generally without accelerating, so that you can have a good, hard look before you commit yourself to passing. Confirm your assessment of the available stretch of road. Check the speed and distance of any oncoming vehicle in the distance. Make sure there are no side turnings or laybys. Observe your return position, in case it contains a hazard which you had not previously seen. This sizing-up process, which you run through very quickly, occurs while your car is still travelling at a similar speed to the vehicle in front, and remains a reasonable distance behind it. If conditions are right, accelerate briskly and make your move. If conditions are not right, slide comfortably back to the left-hand side of the road – normally you will not have to use the brakes if you judge the procedure properly.

The overtaking position (top), the take-off position (centre), and the path towards the return position (bottom).

The return position
This is the third 'corner' of the triangle. It is the 'destination' you aim to reach swiftly and with a relatively straightened line from your wide take-off position. This course will bring you back to the left-hand side of the road at the earliest opportunity, but without cutting too closely in front of the vehicle you have passed.

Common mistakes when overtaking

Overtaking must be postponed here: a vehicle could emerge from the left turn.

Developing good overtaking technique is one of the most challenging areas of driving. Every time you overtake, look back on your manoeuvre and ask yourself whether you could have applied extra precision and judgement to it. This catalogue of common mistakes may help you identify areas for improvement.

- Sitting far too close behind a vehicle while preparing to overtake. It is especially easy to fall into this habit if you have a low-powered car with poor acceleration.
- Waiting in the overtaking position for a chance that is not going to come for a long time, because the road is too twisty or there is too much traffic.
- Forcing other drivers to brake in order to accommodate misjudged, or even reckless, overtaking.
- Using anticipation in the wrong way by taking a 'run-up' before overtaking. This tactic involves charging up behind to gather momentum before ducking out with deft timing the instant an oncoming vehicle has gone past. Many drivers, usually of low-powered cars, think this constitutes skilled overtaking, but it dangerously sacrifices the safe following distance and usually occurs when the overtaking opportunity is marginal.
- Turning a safe opportunity into a risky one through inattention, poor positioning and lack of observation. While they are weighing things up, such drivers let the first part of an opportunity pass before making an ill-judged move at a late stage.
- Using another overtaking car as a shield to go past as well when the situation is marginal. At best this means taking some risk with oncoming traffic, but at worst the second driver can be caught in a serious predicament if the first driver overtakes more slowly than expected.
- Starting to overtake without realising that a faster car or motorcycle is already looming behind on an overtaking course.
- Relying on a degree of optimism when making a 'borderline' decision on quieter roads. Some drivers take a calculated risk, deciding to go if it seems 'fairly unlikely' that an oncoming vehicle will appear at the brow or bend that lies a reasonable, but not totally safe, distance ahead.
- Moving out at the last moment: this tends to impose a course like an exaggerated loop, bringing the driver back in much too late as well.
- Assessing an overtaking possibility so inadequately that the manoeuvre has to be aborted at a very late stage, perhaps when alongside the other vehicle, by braking hard in order to drop back into place.
- When overtaking two vehicles, failing to anticipate that the driver ahead may overtake as well. Difficult situations arise in this way when someone drives like a bully or is simply unaware of the risk.
- Ignoring the presence of junctions, driveways, houses or laybys in the view ahead.
- Failing to observe the 'return position' in front of a lorry, coach or caravan, and finding that another vehicle has to be overtaken as well.

Wet weather

Overtaking obviously becomes more dangerous in bad conditions. The road surface is more treacherous and spray thrown up by traffic reduces visibility. Remember that the reasonable view ahead available when you lie back at the normal following distance can become obscured by a cloud of spray when you move forward to the overtaking position. If most vehicles have their headlights on, be aware of the difficulty of spotting one that does not.

Overtaking is more dangerous in reduced daytime visibility. When most drivers have headlights on, an unlit vehicle can be difficult to spot.

Making overtaking easier for others

If others want to overtake you, try to drive in a helpful way, even if they are travelling too fast for the conditions or breaking the speed limit.

- Leave a particularly generous gap to the vehicle in front. A driver behind is more likely to make a rash move if frustrated by the prospect of having to overtake two vehicles at once.
- Avoid any inclination to compete for an overtaking chance with a more forceful driver behind. It may be irritating to surrender a good opportunity, but it is best to let the other driver go first. Watch the mirrors carefully for a driver in a high-powered car appearing unexpectedly.
- If traffic conditions allow it, try to improve overtaking opportunities for other drivers. Keep your speed down when their chances arise. Tucking yourself a little closer to the nearside will show your intention to co-operate. As long as it is not ambiguous to operate your left-hand indicator briefly, consider this as a further signal.
- If a risky situation develops during an overtaking move, try to change your speed to help the errant driver, by braking or accelerating.

Cross-hatchings

There are some cross-hatchings that are clearly defined as no-go areas by law and these must be avoided at all times in the course of your normal driving. Those bounded by solid white lines – to separate traffic or mark the approach to motorway slip roads – should never be encroached upon except in a serious emergency or if directed there by a police officer.

Cross-hatched central strips bounded by broken lines are used to separate the vehicle streams on some wide trunk roads that might once have been marked with three lanes. It is useful to turn to the *Highway Code* for guidance here: 'Where the line is broken, you should not enter unless you can see that it is safe to do so.'

The sanction implied in the last sentence allows you to consider overtaking – but remember that this white line system is generally used on roads with a bad accident record. Overtake at a moderate pace and in such a way that the drivers you pass are not taken by surprise.

Two-way roads with three lanes

Thankfully the dangers of the old three-lane 'killer' roads have been reduced by the use of cross-hatched central strips (see above) or solid white line systems, but special observation is still needed.

Double white lines confining one traffic stream to a single lane and the other to two lanes prevent any confusion, but often you see a solid line paired with a broken one. Normally these markings are used on hills, and most drivers interpret them as providing centre-lane priority for uphill traffic without preventing downhill traffic from overtaking if the road is clear. Sometimes, but not always, circular 'priority' signs confirm this interpretation, but they do not alter the extraordinary range of legal possibilities – strictly only uphill traffic is prevented from using the third lane.

With or without circular 'priority' signs, these markings must be treated with great caution because of the potential for conflict in the centre lane. Avoid the 'press-on-regardless' approach often seen from drivers using the centre lane as a long-awaited overtaking opportunity. Overtake only when you have a good view, remembering that vehicles you are about to pass will close down the view if the road bends to the left.

Overtaking on dual-carriageways

The overtaking guidance given in the 'Advanced Motorway Driving' section (see page 66) applies to two-lane or three-lane dual-carriageways, but the extra hazards encountered require first-class observation.

Although the speed limit is 70mph unless marked otherwise, bicycles, mopeds and tractors can use these roads. Side turnings do not always have slip roads, broken-down vehicles cannot find refuge on a hard shoulder, vehicles can emerge from laybys, and some junction layouts allow traffic to join or leave a carriageway through the central reservation.

Advanced checklist

- Consider whether you actually need to overtake.
- Ensure that you always overtake safely, without the remotest element of optimism.
- Study the subtleties of the correct overtaking method – the 'overtaking triangle' – and use every overtaking manoeuvre to develop skilful use of it.
- Remember that overtaking safely is one of the most challenging areas of driving, so absorb the list of 'common mistakes' and try to eliminate them from your driving.
- Do not forget how you can also help others to overtake.

What the examiner looks for

- Is overtaking carried out smoothly, decisively and safely?
- Do you position your car well at all stages of an overtaking manoeuvre?
- Are mirror, signals and gears used correctly?
- Do you avoid cutting in sharply after overtaking?
- Do you ever break the speed limit during an overtaking manoeuvre?

Driving in town

The extra demands in town

Sustained concentration and a high degree of observation are required when driving along busy streets.

Driving in built-up areas demands sustained concentration and a high degree of observation. Traffic is heavier, situations change more quickly, buildings and vehicles restrict views, pedestrians need to be watched, and the frequency of road junctions provides many more accident possibilities.

Local knowledge is invaluable in town, although you must always guard against dropping your level of concentration simply because you are driving in familiar territory. Whenever advanced drivers venture to unfamiliar places, however, they consciously record their features in order to remember important junctions, badly congested areas, one-way systems, roundabouts and filter lights.

Whether or not you are driving over known roads, keep trying to observe what is happening to the traffic flow ahead by positioning your car carefully to maximise your view. Watch for the pattern of junctions coming up and get in the correct line of traffic well in advance. If you find yourself stuck in the wrong lane and cannot safely move to the right one, you must keep to your committed path and use your sense of direction to find your way back to the right road.

Guidance to help your drive through heavy urban traffic appears in many parts of this book. Useful sections cover 'Observation' (pages 18-21), 'Junctions' (pages 36-39) and 'Giving signals' (pages 40-42).

Planning your route

Spending a few minutes planning your journey before you set out is always valuable when you drive without a passenger on an unfamiliar route. Write yourself a list of directions which you can consult at a convenient moment, such as when stopped at traffic lights. Normally you can memorise the next two or three instructions to keep you going before the next opportunity to check your notes.

Route notes can be consulted when stopped at traffic lights.

Route observation

Good observation provides you with valuable snippets of information which a less skilled driver would miss. Remind yourself about the points of selective observation covered on page 20.

Keeping an eye on large lorries or buses well down a line of traffic can give you early warning of a halt. Lorries and buses, stationary or moving, can obscure important road signs if you rely on spotting them too late. Delivery vans sometimes park in dangerous places, requiring great care if you need to pass them.

Always be prepared for taxis to move off, stop suddenly or make a U-turn, especially if the 'hire' sign is lit and the cab might be hailed. Shopping streets and railway stations are places where you need to be particularly vigilant for unexpected actions by taxi drivers.

Lines of parked cars also present potential hazards. Choose your course and speed so you can take avoiding action if someone opens a door in your path, and watch for the tell-tale signs – a driver at the wheel, a vibration or puff of smoke from the exhaust, reversing lights lit or front wheels angling out – which reveal that a car is about to pull out.

Leaning cyclist and truck turning through cross-hatchings are particular hazards in this congested scene.

Pedestrians and cyclists

Lines of parked cars or stationary traffic are places where a pedestrian may pop through a gap. You need to be particularly careful where shoppers may step off a crowded pavement, or near particular buildings – schools, factories, railway stations or pubs – where crowds of people may be present at certain times of day.

Special care is needed where pedestrians cross at traffic lights. People often step into the road when they hear the 'green man bleeping' without glancing to see whether it is actually safe to do so. When a large number of pedestrians stream across in front of you it is quite possible that a few 'stragglers' will cross as your lights are changing to green.

You must be alert for pedestrians making sudden movements across the road, perhaps to take advantage of a gap in the traffic without looking carefully enough to notice your presence. Watch for small movements – a turn of the head, a wave or a brisk walk towards the kerb – which may indicate a pedestrian's next move.

Give cyclists plenty of room when you pass, as they may lack road sense and make sudden movements. Beware of the cyclist who emerges from a side street without looking, and never forget that any cyclist is entitled to a wobble, as a High Court ruling has confirmed.

Lane discipline

Lane discipline is vital in the one-way systems used in many larger towns to keep traffic moving.

In really congested conditions which encourage drivers to become more forceful, or even aggressive, you have to be especially careful to look ahead and notice turns out of the system in time to take up position among a stream of nose-to-tail vehicles in the appropriate lane. Keep to the left, unless this lane leads to a mandatory left turn you do not want to follow, or you plan to turn right.

Overtaking is permissible on both sides on one-way streets, but if you pass vehicles on the nearside be alert to the possibility of one of them suddenly moving into your path in order to turn left. Watch out for pedestrian crossings in one-way streets, as these can be obscured by congested traffic.

Lights and zig-zag white lines add visibility to Pelican crossings, but pedestrian crossings without these features can be obscured by traffic when there are two lanes. Overtaking is forbidden – but commonly seen – where there are zig-zag lines.

Road surfaces

Urban road surfaces are usually more slippery because the coating of oil and rubber on streets becomes polished by constant traffic. Special care is needed even in dry weather, but after a shower urban roads can become very tricky.

Oil tends to accumulate on the road at any places where vehicles stop regularly, such as at traffic lights, so allow for the possibility of reduced grip when braking and accelerating. Tight junctions, roundabouts and filling stations are places where you may encounter spilled diesel fuel.

Parking

Step 1. Having sized up the space when passing it, use left steering lock to bring your car close to the rear corner of the parked car ahead.

Step 2. Transfer to right steering lock at the correct moment to bring the nose of your car close to the rear corner of the parked car ahead.

Step 3. At the end of the reversing manoeuvre, your car ends up parallel with the kerb and close to the parked car behind.

Step 4. Centre your car in the space so that the driver of the car behind can extract it from its space.

Although the ability to park in a confined space at the roadside has to be demonstrated during the L-test, it is incredible how inept many people are at executing this basic manoeuvre.

Leaving the car too far from the kerb, at an angle to the kerb or with one wheel over the kerb are common mistakes that result from inability or a 'can't be bothered' attitude. Some drivers try to enter a parking space nose first, while others habitually scrape wheels and tyres against the kerb. Sometimes you see a parking performance which shows that the driver has no idea of the car's dimensions.

Good parking technique enables you to make the most of a small space. Reversing into a space gives you a chance to size up the gap as you drive slowly past it and always gets your car in place more efficiently. Having a good idea of your car's dimensions and timing your steering accurately should see you snugly into a space in a single manoeuvre.

Always aim to park on the left-hand side of a two-way road, even if the first space you see after a long search is on the right. Moving across a stream of oncoming traffic invites danger, and restricted visibility from the driving seat makes it very difficult to emerge from the space again. At night it is illegal to park against the direction of the traffic flow.

A nose-first attempt into the same space – not a hope.

Stopping on hills

Leaving a good gap when stopped in traffic on a hill provides room if the driver ahead makes a poor start and lets the car roll back

Holding a car stationary on a hill with the clutch is a bad habit that many drivers develop after passing their L-test. Apart from being a precarious way of steadying your car, this wears out the clutch quickly. Use the handbrake, and select neutral if you expect to be stopped for more than a few seconds.

When you stop in a queue of traffic on a hill, always allow a little extra room in case the vehicle in front should roll back. The driver may not have applied the handbrake firmly enough, or may make such a clumsy start that the vehicle slips back a metre or so before the clutch bites.

Confidence in congested conditions

Drivers unused to big cities have to adjust to more demanding traffic conditions. Congestion and delay mean that city drivers get a move on when they can, driving in confident, decisive style.

Drivers who are used to the very dense and sometimes fast-moving traffic of large cities are generally more confident. They have a decisive style which seems almost foolhardy to people who normally drive on quieter roads, but by and large it works well because they know what they are doing and where they are going. The 'press-on' approach helps to move large volumes of traffic through congested road systems.

Your driving should be in keeping with your surroundings. Applying a decisive style to gaps in the traffic in a small town can seem aggressive, even reckless, partly because it is out of place. In the same way, someone driving warily in a big city for the first time must try not to be intimidated by cut-and-thrust driving at peak hours.

Each type of progress is right for the conditions, so it can be dangerous if you do not – or even feel that you cannot – conform to the traffic pattern around you.

Advanced checklist

- When driving in town, develop your skills of selective observation to a high pitch because so much more happens around you.
- Extra anticipation is needed to spot unexpected movements from pedestrians, cyclists and parked vehicles.
- Ensure when parking that you reverse into a space with a single, well-judged manoeuvre.
- Leave some space when stopped on a hill to allow for the vehicle in front rolling backwards.

What the examiner looks for

- Are you careful not to obstruct other vehicles, by driving too slowly, taking up the wrong position on the road, or failing to anticipate and react correctly to the traffic situation ahead?
- Do you keep to the correct part of the road, especially when approaching or negotiating hazards?
- Do you keep an eye on the road surface, especially in bad weather, and do you watch out for slippery conditions?
- Are signals, signs and road markings observed, obeyed and approached correctly?
- Do you drive with courtesy, especially at pedestrian crossings?
- Are manoeuvres, such as parking and reversing, performed smoothly and competently?

Driving in the country

Observation on open roads

Country roads have less traffic, but there are all sorts of other hazards. Do not expect much road sense from sheep...

Although the basic rules of advanced driving remain the same in all environments, travelling along open roads needs a different set of abilities.

Country roads give you a chance to enjoy your driving to the full. You can achieve good progress because traffic is light, enjoy cornering at higher speeds, appreciate the scenery and derive satisfaction from making well-judged overtaking manoeuvres.

Your need to assess the road ahead is just as important in the country as in town, but the clues to look for are different. The list is almost endless, but one hallmark of advanced drivers is that they can recognise information useful to them. Some useful hints are given in the section on selective observation (see page 20).

Any livestock in the fields would suggest that you should watch for mud on the road near gateways or farms. The lie of trees and hedges can indicate the steepness of an incline or the angle of a bend before you see the road. Isolated houses are points where you need to take extra care in case people, animals or vehicles appear.

Full advantage should be taken of views of stretches of road in the distance. Sometimes you can string together enough glimpses to spot an overtaking opportunity that most drivers would miss. You can also give yourself early warning of a car approaching on a narrow road if you see it briefly through a gap in the trees or a gateway.

When you drive in the countryside, sooner or later an animal – perhaps a rabbit or a pheasant – will dart into your path. You will naturally want to avoid hitting it, both for its sake and yours, but try not to react too excessively or hastily. Too sharp a swerve or fierce braking could cause you to lose control of your car.

Side turnings

Approaching side turnings is always potentially hazardous when you are driving at higher speeds along open roads, so you should consider reducing your speed when you see notice of a junction ahead.

If necessary, reduce your speed so that you can slow down sufficiently if a vehicle suddenly emerges from the turning, and keep observing the mouth of the junction as you approach. If a vehicle appears, watch for recognition of your presence from the driver and consider 'covering' the brake pedal – moving your right foot across so that it is poised over the pedal – in case you need to react rapidly.

You should aim to spot side turnings at the earliest opportunity. A triangular sign usually, but not always, gives you advance warning, and often you can pick out a signpost to give you the precise location of a turning before you see it. The white lines bordering the road are particularly informative to an observant driver. Broken lines interrupting a solid line warn of a minor turning (perhaps just a driveway or field entrance), often before you actually see it.

Broken lines interrupting the solid line at the side of the road give early notice of a minor 'turning', which may just be a driveway, field entrance or layby.

Road surfaces

Country road surfaces, particularly on smaller roads, can produce many surprises. A series of bends between high walls or hedges can conceal all manner of dangers, such as potholes, mud, deep puddles, streams of water across the road, patches of loose gravel, tightening-radius bends, dead animals, wet leaves and a strange variety of cambers and bumps. Always be ready for the unexpected.

Safe stopping distances

A blind farm entrance and horses in a bend – two examples of unexpected hazards. Drive at a speed which allows you to stop within the distance you can see to be clear.

The lack of traffic on country roads can tempt even experienced drivers into travelling too fast for safety, so always be sure to drive at a speed which allows you to stop within the distance you can see to be clear. Expect a tractor, horses or a herd of cows around every blind bend.

Be careful to maintain a safe stopping distance behind other vehicles. Many drivers are prone to pressing too close, particularly if they generally drive in urban areas where speeds are much lower.

Keep a proper braking distance even if you are overtaken, and do not fall into the trap of allowing an inadequate distance just because you can see round the car in front. Just occasionally, perhaps if another car emerges suddenly from a side turning, the vehicle in front will stop more quickly than you expect. Since so few drivers leave a safe distance, do not take the gap left by others as some sort of standard for yourself. Behind a lorry or a van, you will normally obtain a better view by hanging even further back.

Technique on dual-carriageways

The experienced driver naturally shows good lane discipline on dual-carriageways with two or three lanes. You will use the nearside lane unless you wish to overtake, although when traffic is heavy you may spend much of your time in the centre or right-hand lanes.

Although these roads usually have the same 70mph speed limit as motorways (see pages 62-71), you often encounter an added range of hazards, such as side turnings to the left without slip roads, traffic slowing down in the right-hand lane in order to turn right, and slow-moving vehicles such as tractors or milk floats.

It is not worth seeking the fastest convoys by moving from one lane to another on a busy road: each lane change is an unnecessary danger and frequently offers no advantage.

Advanced checklist

- Absorb all the details of observation and technique appropriate to driving on country roads.
- When driving on open roads develop your skills of selective observation to a high pitch. Often you can identify hazards or spot overtaking opportunities at an early stage.
- Side turnings present potential for danger. Identify them at an early stage, reduce your speed if necessary, watch any waiting vehicles and avoid overtaking.
- Pay special attention to the road surface: slippery surfaces, such as mud, gravel or streams of water, are more common on country roads.
- Although dual-carriageways usually have the same 70mph speed limit as motorways, they present additional hazards such as slow-moving vehicles and side turnings without slip roads.

What the examiner looks for

- Bearing in mind the road, traffic and weather conditions, do you keep up a reasonable pace and maintain good progress?
- Does your driving give evidence of good observation skills?
- Do you exercise caution when approaching side turnings?
- Is your overtaking technique and judgement good?
- Do you keep an eye on the road surface, watching out for slippery conditions?
- Are signals, signs and road markings observed, obeyed and approached correctly?

4 ADVANCED DRIVING IN DIFFICULT CONDITIONS

Driving at night

Seeing and being seen

One of the basic rules of good driving, the need to travel at a speed which enables you to stop within the distance you can see, demands special attention at night. If there is no street lighting, you must be able to pull up within the distance illuminated by your headlights.

On dipped beam along a straight road this may mean that your speed has to be lower at night than during the day. When dropping from main to dipped beam, reduce your speed if necessary to a level appropriate to your shorter range of visibility. If you find your speed creeping up, think of the road debris you occasionally have to steer round during the day – maybe a tyre carcass or dead animal – and imagine what can lie in the darkness ahead.

Drive on main beam whenever the road is unlit and empty. Think about how your headlights are seen by other drivers in choosing the moment when you dip: generally you can stay on main beam a little longer through right-hand bends.

On damp winter roads it is surprising how quickly road grime can coat your headlights. How the unwiped segments of your windscreen look will give you a clue to how much lighting is being lost.

Some benefits of night driving

Driving at night is not all about extra difficulties – it definitely has its advantages. When traffic begins to thin out, a journey can become quicker and less stressful.

Out in the country the ability to see other vehicles, street lighting or even lights from an isolated house in the far distance can give you a 'bigger' picture of the conditions around you. On a twisty road the light thrown by oncoming vehicles gives you early warning of their approach and can help you to assess a bend before you reach it. The extra observation possibilities at night can allow you to find more overtaking opportunities.

At the same time, however, you must resist the temptation to drop your guard during a rewarding night-time drive. It can be difficult to judge speed and distance, so oncoming vehicles can be closer and travelling more quickly than you think.

Different observation possibilities occur at night – light thrown by an oncoming vehicle gives early warning of its approach on a country road.

Checking your lights

Check frequently that all your car's lights work. This is easiest if someone else checks while you run through the switches.

On your own you can cover those functions that cannot be checked while walking round the car – brake lights, reversing lights and headlight flashing – by parking close to a wall and observing the reflected light. When stopped in traffic at night, you can make running checks of your headlights and front indicators by looking for their reflections on the vehicle ahead.

Dazzle

Dazzle in your mirrors is troublesome, but briefly raising your hand to the mirror can be enough to tell a forgetful driver to dip.

Inexperienced drivers sometimes find it difficult to cope with glare from the headlights of oncoming vehicles. Make a conscious effort to look away and concentrate your gaze on your side of the road. With experience this reaction becomes second nature, and you start to appreciate oncoming headlights for the extra light which they throw into your path and the clues they give about the line of the road.

One problem on open roads is that a few inattentive drivers fail to dip their headlights when you approach, although dipping your own beam in good time usually brings the right response. By all means use a quick flash on to main beam to remind another driver to dip, but never stay on main beam in order to retaliate. Two dazzled drivers are twice as dangerous as one.

Remember how the human eye works if you become dazzled. While it can quickly contract the pupil to shut out unwanted light, it takes much longer to dilate afterwards. For several seconds after the vehicle has passed you may be driving with reduced vision.

Dazzle from a vehicle behind can be just as troublesome, although most cars have a 'dipping' interior mirror to relieve this. Remember to return the mirror to its normal position when the dazzle recedes, since a 'dipped' mirror can make a following vehicle look much further away.

Briefly raising your hand in front of the mirror will sometimes bring a response from a forgetful driver, but obviously you cannot do much about a vehicle with a heavy load or misaligned headlights.

Eyesight and fatigue

Any eyesight deficiencies (see page 18) can be relatively worse at night. Dirt on the windscreen, inside or out, makes the task of night observation harder, and in wet weather worn wiper blades can seriously reduce your vision.

Travelling any distance after dark can be more tiring because your eyes have to work harder. You can help to reduce the risk of tiredness by trying to avoid making a long journey at night after a strenuous day. A snack before starting is better than a heavy meal, which might make you feel drowsy. Certainly keep off all alcohol.

Your eyes have to work harder when driving at night, so take a break if fatigue sets in.

Keep asking yourself whether you feel at all tired, and stop for a break if you do. If you think it will help, turn down the heater and open a window to give yourself a blast of cool air until you can find a convenient place to stop.

When you do stop, stretch your arms and legs, and rest your eyes. You could even go for a short but vigorous run up the road to wake yourself up. Carrying a flask of hot coffee or tea can help to restore your senses when a break is necessary.

Take fatigue seriously. A significant proportion of accidents at night occur when a driver nods off to sleep briefly.

Women travelling alone at night

Think whether a journey alone is really necessary. If it is, leave a message with someone giving your estimated time of arrival and telephone them when you have reached your destination. Consider whether your travelling needs might justify the cost of having a mobile 'phone in case your car breaks down.

Stay alert when stopped in traffic and be prepared to move away swiftly in a threatening situation. Keep doors locked and windows shut.

Advanced checklist

- Use dipped and main beam intelligently, and make sure you can always stop safely in the distance illuminated by your headlights.
- Be aware of the difficulties of judging speed and distance at night, particularly when overtaking.
- Make sure all your lights work and are kept clean.
- Carry spare bulbs in case a light fails at night.
- Stop for regular breaks when making a long journey at night. Fatigue is very dangerous; when you begin to feel drowsy your concentration and speed of reaction suffer.

What the examiner looks for

- Do you drive on dipped headlights when conditions require it?

Driving in winter

Ice and snow

In practice, driving can become more hazardous when snow turns to slush. Traffic moves more quickly, but ridges of slush still create difficulty at junctions and when changing lanes.

In freezing conditions it is vital to read the road meticulously so that you anticipate dangerous spots before they catch you out.

If you really cannot avoid driving in snow, go about it with extreme care. The dangers are self-evident and you need to be very cautious in the use of steering, braking and acceleration. You should aim to stay in the highest possible gear to help traction.

In practice the most hazardous conditions tend to occur when snow turns to slush and traffic starts to move more quickly. The feeling of security that can develop when you are able keep to wheel tracks between ridges of slush can tempt you to drive faster than is safe, creating difficulties when you have to turn at a junction or change lanes. Snow and slush always clear less quickly in lanes with less traffic, typically the right-hand lanes, but sometimes you may have to move onto a more slippery surface.

Frost is heaviest late into the night and in the early morning, so the risks are reduced in cold weather if you can make a journey later during the day or in early evening. Try to keep to main roads which have been salted and gritted, and to an extent scoured by traffic, since minor roads may not have been treated in the same way.

Even on a fine day when the road surface seems normal, ice can remain where trees and walls shade the road, where gradients are not warmed by the sun, or where wind sweeps across an exposed hilltop or bridge. Although the roughened texture of many concrete road surfaces with grooves running laterally across the road can offer good grip in dry weather, the water which settles in the grooves can create a very treacherous surface when it freezes.

Expert observation of the road surface is crucial when dealing with isolated patches of frozen road, but keep an eye on other road users as well since their actions can give you advance warning of danger.

Black ice

The notorious hazard of black ice should always be expected on a cold night, and for several hours at least during the following morning. Black ice occurs where water gathers during the day and freezes at night. The road surface looks wet when in fact it is icy – and in some conditions black ice can be virtually invisible.

Because black ice occurs in patches, it is very easy to be lulled into a false sense of security after driving for several miles along a road which seems normal. The only advice must be to drive very cautiously when the temperature is low enough for black ice to be a risk.

Correcting a front-wheel skid

A front-wheel skid makes the car fail to respond to the steering and travel straight on in a corner. This tends to occur in a front-wheel drive car through applying too much power, steering too sharply or braking too heavily, but abrupt steering and braking can have the same effect in rear-wheel drive cars.

To regain control, take your foot off the accelerator and steer smoothly in the direction of the skid. When you feel the tyres bite again, gently steer the car back onto course. Unless your car is fitted with electronic traction control, it may also be useful to disengage the clutch.

Correcting a rear-wheel skid

A rear-wheel skid causes the tail of the car to move sideways, possibly bringing the car into a spin if you fail to correct it. Normally it is caused by using too much power when cornering a rear-wheel drive car, but a front-wheel drive car can also slide at the back if unsettled by a sudden transfer from brisk acceleration to heavy braking.

To regain control, lift off the accelerator and steer in the direction of the skid, so that the front wheels remain pointing in the intended direction of travel.

This technique, called opposite-lock, requires smooth, panic-free steering and good reactions. Many drivers do this instinctively, but avoiding over-correction takes practice and skill.

Getting moving in snow

If you find it difficult to get moving, the answer is to supply minimal power to the wheels. Starting in second gear and releasing the clutch gently will deliver power to the driving wheels with minimum force.

You may find you can move a metre or so before wheelspin bogs you down again. With good sensitivity about traction, you may be able to 'rock' the car free by letting it roll backwards and forwards a few times to create slightly more momentum. But take care not to let wheels spin themselves into a deeper hole.

Digging away snow from in front of the driving wheels will help, and anything that might improve traction – soil, twigs, rags, blankets or even your car's floormats – can make all the difference.

Winter accessories

Take your pick. Some of these cold weather aids may be useful to you, especially if your car is not garaged.

You should keep some basic cold weather aids in your car throughout the winter. A de-icer spray, moisture dispersant, ice scraper, torch and screen wash are among the essentials.

When conditions look very severe, a small shovel could be useful for clearing away snow and spreading grit under the tyres if you run out of grip on a hill. A couple of old blankets carried in the boot might also help provide extra grip for the driving wheels if you become stuck. Additional clothing, wellington boots, some food and a flask of tea or coffee would also be useful.

But do consider carefully whether you need to travel when conditions are bad.

Keeping your windows clear

Windows tend to mist up in bad weather if you fail to make the most of your car's heating and ventilation system. Since setting off on a cold morning is usually the worst time for misting up, make sure your windows are genuinely clear before moving off – but avoid causing unnecessary pollution by leaving the engine running for a long time to warm up the car.

Condensation builds up more quickly if you have several passengers in the car, so it may be necessary sometimes to open the windows a little – just a centimetre should do – to keep plenty of fresh air circulating.

Windscreen wiper blades and washers need to be in good order, and water on exterior mirrors can make rear observation more difficult. Draping newspaper or sacking over the windscreen on a cold night will keep it free of frost.

For a clear view ahead – and in other directions – keep windows clear inside and out. Misting up can occur in cold weather; adding 'screen wash' to the washer bottle will prevent the water freezing.

Advanced checklist

- When roads are slippery, use the controls – brakes, steering, accelerator, clutch – even more smoothly and gently than normal to avoid skidding.
- Read the road to prepare yourself for slippery spots; treat the surface with the utmost respect if black ice is a possibility.
- Be familiar with the procedures for controlling a skidding car: steer into the skid and do not brake. Consider a skidpan course to improve your skills.
- If your car is stuck in snow, use second gear and gentle throttle to avoid wheelspin.
- Make sure your car is prepared for winter.

What the examiner looks for

- Do you keep a good eye on the road surface, especially in bad weather?
- Does your car appear to be well maintained?
- Do you drive with proper restraint and sensitivity of control when roads are slippery?

Driving in fog

Speed and vision

The fundamental rule in fog, as in all other conditions, is to keep your speed down to a level which allows you to stop within the range of your vision, even if this means travelling at only 10mph.

Remember that fog is usually accompanied by a damp road surface. Droplets of moisture can collect almost imperceptibly on the windscreen, so use the wipers every now and then.

The concentration required in fog brings on fatigue and eyestrain much more quickly. Stop for a rest more often than normal on a long journey.

Traffic

Drive at a speed that allows you to stop within the distance you can see to be clear – this advice becomes crucially important in fog.

It is very easy in fog to think that a vehicle ahead of you is moving unnecessarily slowly. But remember that while you can see a pair of red beacons through the fog, the driver ahead may be able to see virtually nothing.

You can also be misled about visibility because a vehicle ahead of you makes a slight 'hole' in the droplets of water which form fog. You may feel that the fog has eased slightly while you are in another vehicle's wake, only to find, when you are committed to an overtaking manoeuvre, that it is as thick as ever. Furthermore you may feel under pressure, once you are in front, to justify your manoeuvre by driving too fast for the conditions. It is much better to keep station and keep calm.

While it is wise to stay in line, do not be tempted to stay in touch with the tail lights of a driver whose speed seems too fast for safety. In the sense of loneliness which accompanies fog it can be reassuring to travel in the presence of other vehicles, giving your eyes some relief from the strain of peering through the gloom, but do so only in a manner which is safe for the conditions.

Being seen

Dipped headlights must be used when visibility drops to 100 metres, but in practice you will switch them on long before this. It is better to avoid using main beam, because fog reflects so much light that dipped beam generally gives you a better view.

High-intensity rear foglights should be switched on when traffic is light and fog is very thick, but bear in mind their disadvantages (see page 69).

Junctions are always hazardous in fog, particularly right turns, so flash your headlights on to main beam and sound your horn when you have to cross the path of other vehicles. You are at greater risk while turning at a right angle across a road because your front and rear lights cannot be seen so easily by an oncoming driver. Besides all the usual careful observation, wind down a window and try to listen for approaching vehicles.

Patchy fog

Fog can occur in patches, sometimes unexpectedly. Pockets of it sometimes linger in valleys on a country road, even in summer. Sea fog can occur on coastal roads. If the cloudbase is low you can suddenly find yourself in fog on high ground. Fog tends to form first over water, so if mist develops expect thicker patches where the road crosses a river.

Good observation should always prepare you for patches of fog. Drop your speed and use dipped headlights.

Advanced checklist

- Reduce your speed in fog so you can stop within the distance you can see, even if this means you drive at only 10mph. Postpone or abandon a journey if conditions are very bad.
- In fog dipped headlights tend to give better vision than main beam.
- Be cautious in traffic: avoid overtaking, since visibility may be worse than you think; do not stay in touch with a car which is travelling too fast; always allow enough space so that you can stop safely if the vehicle ahead stops instantaneously in a collision.
- Remember that fog makes the road surface damp and coats your windscreen with moisture.

What the examiner looks for

- Do you drive at an appropriate speed if visibility is reduced?
- Do you leave a safe distance behind vehicles in front?

Driving in summer

Road surfaces

A film of dust, rubber and oil accumulates on roads during dry weather. This does not greatly affect grip while the road remains dry, but a summer shower or morning dew can make this greasy coating very slippery. The longer a dry spell, the more treacherous the roads can be when rain does come.

Be particularly careful at roundabouts, junctions, in towns and through bends on roads where traffic is heavy. After a while this coating is washed away by rain and the surface becomes less slippery.

Summer is also the time of 'loose chippings'. Dressed with a layer of tar and stone chippings, such roads need to be treated cautiously because grip is greatly reduced and stones are thrown up by other vehicles.

Holiday traffic

Extra awareness is needed to escape the antics of other drivers on busy routes during school holidays and bank holiday weekends. These are situations where you see some very bad driving. The typical holiday driver is hot and bothered, unused to lon[illegible] journeys, frustrated by del[illegible]cted by fractious children, [illegible]le to see properly out of an overloaded car. Expect the unexpected from such drivers.

Obscured vision

Never be lazy about cleaning off the squashed insects and grease which accumulate on your windscreen so quickly in summer. Your vision is impaired in the dry, but can become virtually obliterated if you have to use the wipers during a sudden shower. The wipers will do a better job if you add 'screen wash' to the reservoir, but also clean the windscreen before you start your journey and when you stop for fuel.

Summer rain

Look for evidence of the depth of the water before attempting to drive through a deep ford or standing water. Dry out the brakes afterwards by pumping the pedal a few times.

Rain sometimes falls so heavily in a summer shower or thunderstorm that large puddles quickly form, perhaps where drains are blocked. If this looks likely, slow down to a pace which allows you to cope if suddenly faced with several inches of water in conditions of reduced visibility. Braking will need particular care (see pages 31-33).

Rain sometimes falls so heavily that fords become impassable and roads become flooded in dips. Look for evidence of the depth of the water, perhaps by waiting for a braver driver to venture through. If in any doubt, turn round and find another route along nearby roads.

If you decide to press on, use first gear and keep the engine revs up, slipping the clutch if necessary. Drive slowly and evenly so your car does not create a bow wave. Once clear of the flood, dry out the brakes by pumping the pedal a few times.

Advanced checklist

- When roads are slippery, use the controls – brakes, steering, accelerator, clutch – even more smoothly and gently than normal to avoid skidding.
- Allow for greasy roads and poor visibility when rain falls after a long dry spell, and take special care on loose chippings or hot tar.
- Watch out for poor driving standards in busy holiday traffic.

What the examiner looks for

- Do you show awareness of road surface changes?
- Is your windscreen clean?
- Do you drive with proper restraint and sensitivity of control when roads are slippery?

5 ADVANCED MOTORWAY DRIVING

Joining and leaving the motorway

Joining a motorway

Use firm acceleration on the slip road in order to match your speed to the motorway flow in the left-hand lane.

The motorway slip road should be used to accelerate to a speed which matches that of traffic in the left-hand lane. Consider a right-turn signal so that anyone in the left-hand lane has extra confirmation of your presence. If traffic allows it, a thoughtful driver will move to the centre lane to give you plenty of room.

Your run along the acceleration lane should be timed so that you slip neatly into place as soon as possible without losing speed, but keep a wary eye on the timid driver who may be slowing down at the end of the slip road to wait for a larger gap in the traffic. In extreme cases, this kind of driver – as much a menace to themselves as to other road users – may even stop at the end of the slip road as if to give way.

Joining a motorway needs alert all-round observation to assess the situation on the slip road as well as on the motorway itself. Keep a good eye on your mirrors, but just before you join the carriageway you should glance over your right shoulder to make sure you have not missed a vehicle lurking in a mirror blindspot. Make sure you are a safe distance behind other vehicles when you take your eyes off the road ahead for this instant.

Advanced driving is all about total awareness, and sometimes you can find opportunities to plan your course even before venturing on the slip road. A good example is when the motorway is approached by a bridge or an embankment. If you assess traffic in advance correctly, you will find it easier to blend smoothly with it from the slip road. If you see a hold-up, you can decide whether to change your route to ordinary roads.

You should remain in the left-hand lane until you have adjusted yourself to motorway speeds and assessed the traffic pattern around you.

Your cruising speed will probably mean that you spend a good proportion of your motorway journey in the centre lane, so move over (after the usual mirror and shoulder check and right-turn signal) when it becomes necessary. Return to the left-hand lane whenever it is reasonably clear after overtaking has been completed.

Difficult approaches

When a slip road climbs, your observation has to be sharper because you have less time to assess the state of play on the motorway. Urban motorways can create added problems because congested conditions make it less likely that nose-to-tail vehicles in the left-hand lane can move across to give you room. Some urban motorways also have unhelpfully short slip roads, requiring you to be even more alert and decisive in your actions.

Avoid getting involved in the jostling that can occur on a busy slip road. Some mindlessly aggressive drivers treat the slip road as an opportunity to muscle past a few cars with slower acceleration and veer onto the motorway before the vehicles around them, ignoring the fact that they can pass hundreds of people safely once they are on the motorway. This behaviour puts extra pressure on your observation, so concentrate hard and expect surges of acceleration from the faster cars around you.

Traffic on slip roads is increasingly segregated by strips of cross-hatching with a solid border. You must not cross these areas except in an emergency. Take up your position at an early stage, using the 'lane of least resistance' if lane instructions give you a choice. Sometimes this may be the left-hand lane, which will join a good distance further on, but the right-hand lane is better if there are heavy lorries about.

Where a slip road is segregated by cross-hatchings, choose the 'lane of least resistance'.

Leaving a motorway

Junction signs are normally posted 1 mile and ½ mile in advance, followed by three-, two- and one-bar signs which provide a countdown starting at 300 yards. You must synchronise your speed with the traffic in the left-hand lane, making sure you have moved into this lane by the time you reach the three-bar sign, or earlier in heavy traffic. The right time to start your left-turn signal is at the three-bar sign.

Caution is needed on the slip road. After driving for maybe a couple of hours at close to the legal limit, your judgement of speed will have become distorted. Since 50mph can seem more like 30mph, it is easy to approach the roundabout or junction at the end of the slip road too quickly and end up having to brake heavily. Some slip roads curve so sharply that the dangers of misjudging your speed become even greater. Keep an eye on the speedometer and the movement of vehicles in your mirrors.

Good mirror observation is needed when you leave the motorway, particularly if you plan to take the right-hand lane on the slip road. The type of reckless driver who lunges across from the right-hand lane to the motorway exit at the last moment can take you by surprise.

After the higher pace of the motorway, exit slip roads demand very careful judgement of speed, especially when they bend sharply.

Be prepared for the driver who cuts across your bows at the last moment before an exit.

Advanced checklist

- When joining a motorway, use the slip road to accelerate to a speed which matches the flow in the left-hand lane, maintaining good lane discipline.
- Use good mirror observation to assess the traffic conditions on the motorway as you approach; glance over your shoulder to check any blindspots before you move onto the motorway.
- Move to the left-hand lane in good time when preparing to leave a motorway.
- Be careful not to underestimate your speed when approaching the junction at the end of an exit slip road.

What the examiner looks for

- Do you show good judgement when joining a motorway, with proper use of mirrors and positioning, and awareness of traffic flows?
- Can you use acceleration on the slip road to blend well with traffic in the left-hand lane?
- Do you return to the left-hand lane and signal in good time before leaving the motorway?
- *Note: not all test routes can include motorway evaluation.*

On the motorway

Concentration and observation

Motorways lack many of the features that keep your mind alert. The view is monotonous, the road tends to be straight, and scenery is often shut out by embankments or fences. You also have less work to do controlling your car – steering, changing gear, accelerating, braking – on a motorway. It is all too easy for the mind to wander, especially when traffic is light.

But advanced driving keeps the mind interested. A tiresome journey is turned into a mobile chess game, selecting course to anticipate the traffic ahead and behind, constantly monitoring speeds and distances of all nearby vehicles, and watching for merging vehicles at junctions.

A typically busy motorway scene, with many drivers – particularly those in the right-hand lane of the oncoming carriageway – travelling far too close together.

An advanced driver's progress is planned, smooth, safe and unobtrusive.

Lane discipline

Poor lane discipline in busy conditions: the heaviest traffic is in the right-hand lane, yet much of the left-hand lane is empty.

Maintaining strict lane discipline means that you are always in the appropriate lane for your speed and the traffic conditions. Glance in the mirrors frequently so that you are constantly aware of the relative speeds of all the vehicles around you. Return to the left when you can, but do not do this so over-zealously that you end up constantly skipping from one lane to another.

Poor lane discipline is probably the worst feature of motorway driving in Britain, and it can occasionally play its part in an accident by causing frustration and unnecessary lane-changing, and by shifting too much traffic into the right-hand lane. Far too often on motorways you see strings of cars bunched needlessly in the right-hand lane, queueing up to pass a few people drifting along in the centre lane.

If you come up behind a 'lane hog' who fails to move over when there is plenty of space available, do not resort to aggressive tactics or attempt to teach a lesson. Flashing your headlights, tailgating or sounding your horn is not the way to get lane hogs to move over, and can often make them more stubborn. The principles of advanced driving require you to maintain a proper braking distance, so be patient and wait for an opportunity to overtake safely. Making a point by slicing across a lane hog's bows after you pass is silly, and overtaking on the inside is illegal.

Poor lane discipline in quiet conditions: the typical 'middle lane hog', ignoring the empty left-hand lane stretching far ahead.

Speed

Your speed should be a steady pace at which you and your car feel comfortable, and one which is appropriate to weather conditions and traffic density – but it should not be over 70mph.

Travelling slightly below the limit will save fuel and make little difference to your journey time, and may be more relaxing if you have a long stretch on the motorway ahead of you. Travelling above the limit is definitely not relaxing, if only because you will have to keep watching your mirrors for an ominous blue flashing light. Keep checking the speedometer because your speed can creep up unnoticed and your judgement of braking distance can lapse.

It seems inevitable that automatic cameras will be used increasingly on sections of motorway that have a bad speeding record. It is a sobering thought that a driver could trigger off several cameras on a single journey if speed limits are completely disregarded.

Sunny day, fast car, not much traffic around – but the 70mph speed limit must still be obeyed.

Keeping your distance

An appalling example of 'tailgating'. At this mindless following distance the offending driver's view ahead is completely obscured.

The need to keep a safe distance behind the vehicle in front takes on added importance on a motorway. As the sensation of speed inevitably becomes dulled, it is all too easy to close up so that the distance between you is nothing like adequate in an emergency. Keep reminding yourself of this, by checking the speedometer if it helps to bring home the point.

Many drivers find it difficult to remember the stopping distances quoted on the back page of the *Highway Code*. At 70mph thinking distance of 21 metres and braking distance of 75 metres give a total stopping distance of 96 metres, or 24 car lengths. As a handy reminder, the IAM recommends a 'two second rule', whereby you allow a gap which keeps you a minimum of two seconds behind the vehicle in front. Even this is barely enough: two seconds at 70mph gives you only 62 metres.

You are deluding yourself if you think that driving within this safe distance is acceptable because you can see several vehicles ahead. This attitude ignores all kinds of possibilities: the driver ahead might brake unexpectedly if something lying in the road is seen, a vehicle from the opposing carriageway could crash through the central reservation, or the vehicle a little way ahead might even suffer a tyre blow-out.

Despite being extremely dangerous, 'tailgating' is often seen on motorways. Whatever the reason – aggression or lack of awareness – it is completely unacceptable. Dealing with aggressive 'tailgaters' is simply a matter of letting them by at the earliest opportunity because they inevitably want to travel faster than the flow. If you feel tormented by the sort of absent-minded 'tailgater' who holds station through your lane changes and simply sits too close, decide whether you can best shake off this menace by speeding up or moving to the left-hand lane and slowing down sufficiently for the driver to wake up and overtake.

On a congested motorway it becomes very difficult to preserve a safe braking distance. You just have to do your best, which will always be a compromise. When an overtaking vehicle slots into the adequate gap you have allowed, ease off the accelerator for a moment and drop back accordingly.

Keeping your distance enables you to cope comfortably with the occasions when you see a firework display of brake lights and the traffic flow comes to a sudden halt. Be aware, however, of the vehicles behind you and try to brake progressively if they seem too close. Using the hazard warning lights, a common motorway practice these days, can usefully reinforce the message given by your brake lights.

Changing lanes and overtaking

Good forward observation and alertness always gets you into the desired lane at an early stage.

Take special care with your mirror observation, sizing up the movements of vehicles behind you, when planning a lane change to overtake. Signal in good time when a safe opportunity arises, make your lane change gradually and increase your speed if necessary. Judge your move so that you never impede a faster vehicle.

Sometimes you can reasonably invite co-operation from drivers behind you. If you are in the left-hand lane and a driver coming up in the centre lane can safely make space for you by moving across, give an early signal and move when you have seen a reaction. But do not expect co-operation, or request it where it cannot be given comfortably.

Changing lanes to overtake in heavy motorway traffic requires your best powers of observation. Frequent checking in your mirrors is needed to spot a safe gap at an early stage and your signal should be timed accurately. You will often need to accelerate to blend with a faster flow, but take care not to compromise your safe following distance – or anyone else's – when you make your move.

When pulling out from the left-hand lane to the centre lane, be aware of any driver who is completing an overtaking manoeuvre in the right-hand lane and may be about to take the same space, probably without signalling.

Your signal should always be given to inform, not to issue an order (see page 40). Often on congested motorways you will see inexpert or aggressive drivers signal to announce that they are about to muscle into your lane, come what may. On other occasions you will encounter a driver sitting behind another vehicle's bumper and mindlessly signalling away a wish to move into a congested lane, expecting someone magically to create space.

Watch out for these people and anticipate their actions. By constantly monitoring the speeds and distances of everyone around you, you can drive with the blend of courtesy and planning which is one of the hallmarks of the advanced driver. If you can, move across to a right-hand lane at an early stage when you come up on someone who will need to move into your lane. If traffic commits you to staying where you are, try to open up a convenient gap for the other driver, using good judgement to decide whether you accelerate or ease off.

To avoid any chance of being caught unawares by a car travelling in your mirror blindspot, glance over your shoulder before changing lanes.

You should always be aware of the pattern of traffic in your mirrors, but a lapse in concentration might make you forget about a vehicle holding station in a blindspot just behind you. Glance briefly over your shoulder before changing lanes.

Some drivers signal left out of habit at the end of every overtaking manoeuvre, whereas others never do it. The advanced driver's use of this signal lies between these extremes, in any circumstances when it will give useful information to other drivers. The most common occasion occurs when you return to the centre lane in busy traffic at a moment when a driver in the left-hand lane could be about to make an unsignalled move into the same lane. It can also be useful to confirm your intentions to a driver breathing down your neck.

The heavy congestion on some motorways at peak hours means that traffic in the right-hand lanes sometimes moves more slowly than in the left-hand lanes. The *Highway Code* has some advice which you can take provided you apply common sense. Rule 102 says, 'Do not overtake on the left unless traffic is moving slowly in queues and vehicles in a lane on the right are moving more slowly than you are.'

Provided this advice is not used for blatant queue-hopping, it allows you to remain in a left-hand lane, with the safety benefit of more space around you, and move gradually past a slower stream to your right.

Slip road courtesy

Slip road courtesy in action: a driver moves towards the centre lane to make room for the car that is about to join the main carriageway.

As you approach and pass an entrance slip road, keep an eye on traffic about to join the motorway. If it is safe for you to move from the left-hand lane to the centre lane without worrying a driver coming up behind, it is considerate to do so in order to make life easier for the driver joining the motorway, as well as to keep yourself out of trouble.

This forethought will be especially appreciated by lorry drivers, who are less able to adjust their speed to blend into the traffic flow. If a slip road is very busy, this tactic is particularly appropriate.

Do you need a break?

Motorways are invariably the fastest, safest and most convenient route, but over long distances they become dull and fatigue can set in. You should build in enough time on your journey to allow for regular stops to stretch your limbs, rest your mind, and have a hot drink and a bite to eat.

Sometimes it may suit you to 'take a break' on some normal roads to remind you that driving can be enjoyable. Many motorways run reasonably parallel to the trunk roads they were designed to supersede, so you can generally find one or two cross-country sections where you can leave the motorway without travelling any extra distance or risking being held up in towns. Careful study of your road atlas, indeed, can sometimes reveal country roads where you can cut a corner between two different motorways.

At the first sign of drowsiness on a motorway, do something about it. Open the windows, turn the heater to 'cold', switch the heater fan to its fastest setting, and turn on the radio. Feeling sleepy is not an acceptable reason for stopping on the hard shoulder, so keep yourself going until you can leave the motorway at the next exit.

Advanced checklist

- Treat the 70mph speed limit as a limit, not a target that you must reach.
- Remember two essential rules of motorway driving: maintain a safe following distance and exercise good lane discipline.
- Be sure not to let your concentration lapse if your journey becomes monotonous.
- Use good observation and anticipation to fit in comfortably with other traffic when you change lanes.

What the examiner looks for

- Is the speed limit observed?
- Do you follow other vehicles at a safe distance?
- Are your lane discipline, signalling and mirror observation to a high standard?
- Do you concentrate well?
- Do you judge speed and distance well, allowing you to anticipate the movements of other vehicles?

Bad weather

Adjusting to poor conditions

Warm sunshine one minute, a hailstorm followed by fierce winds and heavy rain the next. Britain's notorious weather can pose problems on the motorway.

Think carefully about prevailing traffic conditions when the weather turns nasty. Exactly how you drive depends on the weather you face, but cut your speed, leave longer braking distances, use the smoothest techniques to control your car, increase your concentration, and read the road well, scanning as far ahead as visibility allows.

If it is cold and damp, ensure that you keep the windows demisted. Chatting passengers and a blaring radio may distract you. Do not hesitate to use dipped headlights.

Reduce speed and open up your braking distance when weather conditions deteriorate.

Heavy rain

Heavy rain tends to reduce visibility more on motorways than on ordinary roads. Water drains less easily because the carriageways are not usually cambered, speeds are higher and traffic is often dense.

The spray thrown up by all vehicles in wet weather seriously impairs visibility and inevitably requires that you reduce speed. Trucks are a particular problem because they create huge clouds of spray that can virtually eliminate your view if you try to overtake. Switching your windscreen wipers to their fastest speed will help as you go past, but in very poor conditions it is better to be patient and drop back to a safe following distance.

Aquaplaning is always a danger in heavy rain, particularly if you are travelling too fast. This condition occurs when your car's tyre treads cannot cut through surface water, leaving the car to plane along like a speedboat. You will feel this through the steering wheel: the steering may tug as the front wheels hit the water, and it will certainly feel strangely light.

You should regain control fairly quickly if you hold a straight course, stay off the accelerator and brake pedals, and resist the urge to panic. If, on the other hand, you hit a substantial patch of water while changing lanes, you could be in real trouble. Reduce your speed drastically if standing water builds up, and remember that localised subsidence of the surface can cause pools of water to collect.

Motorway fog

A multiple pile-up on a fogbound motorway occurs almost every winter because so many drivers travel too fast and too close together for the conditions.

As long as so much bad driving persists, always consider whether you want to continue on a motorway if you feel uneasy in fog, whether it is in patches or a blanket. You may be safer on ordinary roads, or it may be best to stop altogether.

The way you drive in motorway fog should be governed by the rules about coping with fog on other roads (see page 60). Keep down to a speed which gives a safe braking distance within your range of vision, try to keep to the left-hand or centre lanes, and ensure that you drive on dipped headlights (plus front foglights if your car has them). High-intensity rear lights should also be used if the fog is really dense and traffic is light.

Remember that an obstruction in front, when you do spot it, may not be another vehicle trundling along a little slower than you. It could be the back of a stationary truck or car, already involved in an accident and possibly unlit.

Strong winds

Motorways are often built up on embankments and are therefore more exposed to wind than ordinary roads. Higher speeds increase the effects of crosswinds and turbulence, which can cause particularly unnerving moments of instability in your car when passing heavy lorries.

It is not just your vehicle which may be affected. Make allowance for other vehicles, particularly those with high sides such as caravans, coaches and trucks. Try to give them a wider berth than normal when overtaking, perhaps by leaving the centre lane free as an extra margin when traffic is light.

Be ready to react if strong winds mean that turbulence from large vehicles could push your car off course.

Ice and snow

Although a threat of freezing temperatures always brings gritting lorries instantly into action on motorways, danger can still lurk at motorway bridges and on less heavily used slip roads. Besides driving at an appropriate speed and leaving good braking distance, make allowances for this by using gentle steering movements and light braking. In short, do not risk any action that might provoke a slide.

Snow is an altogether different matter. First, ask yourself whether your journey is necessary. If it is, ensure you have plenty of fuel, carry a shovel and grippy matting, pack some warm clothing and refreshment, and drive as if you are trying to walk on eggs without breaking them. Staying in as high a gear as possible will reduce the chance of accelerator movement leading to loss of traction.

Observe the road surface very carefully if you are travelling while it is snowing. Try to keep to the left-hand lane once snow starts to settle, since weight of traffic will tend to clear the surface. Certainly avoid the right-hand lane, which is always the first to become impassable. When snow or slush accumulates in ridges between lanes, avoid putting your wheels on these areas unless you absolutely have to.

Headlights and foglights

Most drivers wisely switch on dipped headlights as soon as visibility deteriorates, but there are always exceptions. A vehicle on parking lights or no lights at all is very difficult to spot in gloomy conditions, so look very carefully in your mirrors when you change lanes.

Drivers of cars with front foglights are sometimes too over-enthusiastic in using them. Except when visibility is dramatically reduced by fog or falling snow, having these lights blazing on the front of your car is illegal and causes unnecessary dazzle, making it more difficult for drivers ahead of you to judge your speed and distance.

High-intensity rear foglights are a mixed blessing on motorways. They should be used when conditions are particularly poor and traffic is light, but think carefully about whether they are really beneficial before switching them on.

The long-range visibility offered by high-intensity rear foglights is usually inappropriate in thick traffic and conditions of moderate visibility. The dazzle they cause is annoying and distracting, judging distances is more difficult, their brightness can mask the visibility of brake lights, and other vehicles become less conspicuous. In congested traffic a sudden glimpse of bright red beacons a few cars ahead can make you think the driver is braking heavily – this is a significant and unnecessary cause of danger. And there are always a few people who forget to switch these lights off when visibility improves.

Avoid using front foglights and high-intensity rear lights at night unless visibility is seriously reduced – the dazzle they cause makes speed and distance more difficult to judge.

Advanced checklist

- Drop your speed and allow more stopping distance when weather conditions deteriorate.
- Use the controls with extra smoothness when the road surface is more slippery than usual.
- Be alert to the dangers of fog, leaving the motorway if necessary.
- Use your car's lights thoughtfully, resisting the temptation to switch on front fog lights and high-intensity rear lights unless visibility is very poor.

What the examiner looks for

- Is appropriate restraint shown in bad weather?
- Do you show awareness of the need to reduce speed and open up braking distances in adverse conditions?

Roadworks and breakdowns

Motorway warning signals

Automatic motorway signals give you a recommended maximum speed in bad weather, congested traffic or on the approach to an incident, as well as giving warning of lane closures ahead or even the need to stop or leave the motorway in the event of a serious accident.

Some drivers ignore these signals, believing they have been left on by mistake if no obvious need for them can be seen. It is worth confirming, therefore, that the police are extremely diligent in employing these signals when they are necessary and in switching them off again as soon as danger is cleared. Always obey them, because they invariably warn that a hazard does exist, perhaps a mile or two down the carriageway.

Recently a new type of motorway sign has been installed in many areas. It uses a matrix of lights which can spell out more detailed messages, giving advance warning of congestion, road works or accidents. The messages tend to be more up to the minute on these signs and it is as well to do as they instruct or advise.

Experiments continue into ways of dealing with congestion on motorways. Busy sections of the M25 and M6, for example, are controlled by temporary speed limits at peak periods.

Conspicuously indicated on overhead gantrys, these limits – typically 50mph or 60mph – are designed to 'calm' the traffic flow and eliminate the familiar stop-go phenomenon that occurs when congestion builds up.

Temporary speed limits are used at peak periods on a few busy sections of motorway.

Roadworks and contraflows

Roadworks and contraflows are a familiar part of the motorway landscape these days. By and large the design of coning-off systems, lane restrictions and carriageway changes is excellent, and advance warning is normally given at least a mile ahead, but restraint and planning is needed during your approach to them.

Make any lane change in good time, avoiding the late pushing and shoving into the traffic flow that you sometimes see from press-on-regardless drivers. These tactics can trigger a train of ever-increasing braking from a row of vehicles, sometimes bringing traffic to a standstill. We have all experienced occasions when the motorway flow inexplicably comes to a complete halt, simply because one thoughtless driver cuts in at the last moment.

Speed through contraflows is usually restricted to 50mph, but the way limits are applied is not consistent throughout the country. Obey the signs you see and make sure you preserve your safe following distance when the motorway is congested. Watch out for narrowed lanes, awkward cambers where a contraflow takes you through the central reservation, and poor surfaces when the hard shoulder is pressed into service.

Make any lane change in good time before roadworks and obey reduced speed limits through them.

Traffic information

Bulletins about motorway accidents and serious delays are regularly given out on national and local radio stations. On some motorways the frequencies of local radio stations are given on signposts. Before you travel, Ceefax and Teletext can be useful sources of information about traffic conditions.

The hard shoulder

Motorway breakdowns are sometimes caused by factors which a diligent driver can avoid. Analysis of motorway accidents has shown that one in six is caused by tyre failure, so pay good attention to the pressure and condition of your tyres. If you have an ageing car, ensure that its engine can cope with continuous high speed or a prolonged hold-up: from time to time it pays to check the condition of the radiator, water hoses, engine oil and other fluid levels.

If you are ever forced to stop on a motorway, pull over to the far left of the hard shoulder (use of the hard shoulder, of course, is permissable only in an emergency). Operate your hazard warning lights as a warning to other drivers. Either stay with your car to wait for a police patrol vehicle or start walking to the nearest emergency telephone. Red arrows on the marker posts (at 100-metre intervals) indicate the direction of the nearest one, which will never be more than half a mile away.

Collisions very occasionally occur between motorway traffic and vehicles on the hard shoulder, so in most circumstances it is safest to wait on the verge well back from the carriageway. However, a woman on her own at night, or even in the daytime, is probably better advised to sit in her car with the doors locked until assistance arrives. Having a mobile 'phone is useful in emergencies.

If you are able to resume your journey, do not pull straight on to the main carraigeway after moving off. Treat the hard shoulder as an acceleration lane, making your move to the left-hand lane of the motorway only when your speed matches that of the vehicles around you.

Advanced checklist

- Motorway warning signals are always illuminated for a reason: obey them at all times.
- Make any lane change in good time when approaching roadworks or contraflows.
- Pay proper attention to safety if your car breaks down and you have to stop on the hard shoulder.
- Use the hard shoulder as an acceleration lane when moving away again.

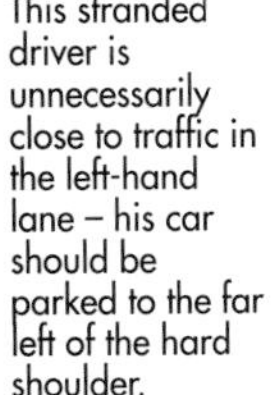

This stranded driver is unnecessarily close to traffic in the left-hand lane – his car should be parked to the far left of the hard shoulder.

What the examiner looks for

- If you encounter bad weather, roadworks or an emergency during your test, how well do you cope?

6 ADVANCED ADVICE FOR YOUR DRIVING CAREER

Accidents

Stop and think

Police, fire and ambulance services are all present at a serious motorway accident blocking the whole carriageway

Everyone hopes never to be involved in a road accident, but the chances of avoiding one throughout your driving life are quite small. It is worth taking a little trouble, therefore, to learn what to do if the worst does occur. Sooner or later you are also likely to arrive at the scene of someone else's accident.

Many things have to be done at once at an accident. You must protect the site from further accidents until the emergency services arrive, warn other drivers, call for assistance and help casualties. Your actions in these first few minutes could be a matter of life and death. Think about what you do: casualties who are unable to move could be more seriously hurt if you try to pull them from a crashed car.

Do not park where your car could be a hazard to traffic. The best place is at the roadside where it can be seen easily by approaching drivers. At night, position the car to illuminate the scene of the accident, but not so that it cannot be seen by drivers.

Switch off the crashed vehicle's engine and disconnect the battery; apply the handbrake and chock the wheels if this seems necessary. Make sure no-one in the vicinity is smoking.

Approaching drivers need plenty of time and distance to slow down. Running into the road and waving your arms wildly could confuse others and put yourself in danger. Instead, run back along the side of the road for at least 100 metres, or until the accident is going out of view. Make a clear 'slow down' signal by moving your arm vigorously up and down, with palm face down, and point decisively to the accident scene. On bends it may be useful to recruit a second person.

Someone should guide vehicles round the accident. Stand in the headlights of a car or under a streetlamp at night, and remember that it will help to wear a pale or reflective garment. Hold a white handkerchief, or better still a torch, to draw extra attention to yourself.

Summoning help

Sending for help is a priority. If this means leaving casualties unattended, get someone else to telephone the emergency services. If no-one else is around you must do this yourself.

When you dial 999 it is vital to provide precise information for the emergency services. Work out your answers to the essential questions. What is the exact location (look for an obvious landmark if you do not know) and, if appropriate, direction of travel? How many casualties are there and how serious are their injuries? Are the casualties trapped? Is the accident causing danger? How many vehicles are involved? Are they cars? Lorries? Tankers? Buses or coaches? Is a traffic jam developing? Are petrol or chemicals spilling?

Tell the operator your telephone number and ask for fire brigade, police or ambulance; you will be connected to each in turn if all three are required. Ask for *Fire Brigade* if there are people trapped, petrol or chemicals on the road, or risk of fire. Ask for *Police* if there are casualties, danger or obstruction to traffic. Ask for *Ambulance* if there are casualties.

Then return immediately to the accident scene to help.

Helping casualties

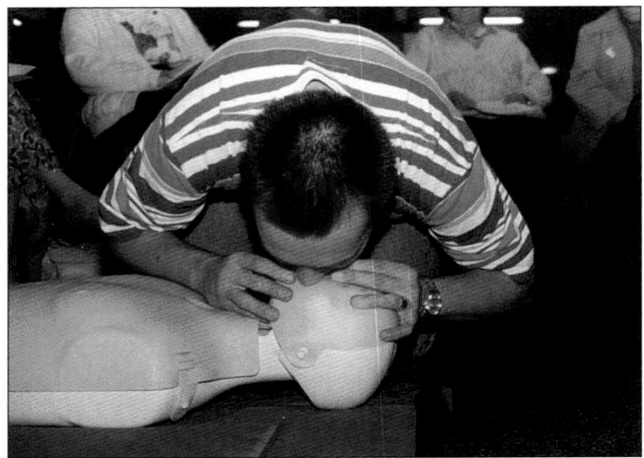

Basic first aid training will teach you life-saving techniques such as mouth-to-mouth resuscitation.

Only move injured people if there is immediate danger, since you could aggravate internal, back or neck injuries. Make sure the person can breathe. Inspect the inside of the mouth and back of the throat. To avoid the danger of choking, remove any food or false teeth. If you cannot detect breathing, attempt mouth-to-mouth resuscitation.

Place the casualty on his or her back, and support the neck so the head falls back to open the airway. Pinch the nose shut and hold the mouth open. Cover the mouth with yours, and blow firmly to inflate the lungs. Then release the nose and mouth. Keep repeating the procedure until the casualty starts to breathe spontaneously.

If the casualty is unconscious, move him or her gently into the 'recovery' position to avoid choking on the tongue or gorging. This involves turning the casualty gently on his or her side and bending arms and legs to keep this position. Straighten and turn the head to one side, facing slightly downwards.

If there is serious bleeding, apply firm pressure to the bleeding point to stem the flow of blood. Use a pad or apply a sterile dressing and bandage firmly. Look for limb fractures and try to stop these limbs moving. If a casualty is sitting up and in no immediate danger, do not make him or her leave the car. Support the head to prevent choking in case he or she passes out.

Keep all casualties warm, including shock cases, but do not give them any pain relievers, alcohol, other drinks, food or cigarettes – they may have internal injuries.

If you are not sure what to do, leave casualties alone provided they are breathing and not bleeding heavily.

This section can give only the most elementary first aid advice, but if you are trained you can clearly help more effectively. The British Red Cross Society or the St John Ambulance Association can advise you.

Removing a motorcyclist's helmet

There is considerable controversy over the need to remove the full-face helmet of an injured motorcyclist, but there is a simple guideline that any rider would like to see observed.

If the rider is breathing and there is no danger of choking, leave the helmet on. If the rider is unconscious and is clearly not breathing, his or her brain will start to die from oxygen starvation in four minutes. The stark choice is then made for you. Would you prefer to try to preserve life or just stand by? If the following advice is used for removing a full-face helmet, you will minimise the risk of further injury.

Unfasten the chin strap before you attempt to remove the helmet. Most UK straps are of the D-ring type, but others have a fastener that works like a seat belt buckle, with a catch that must be pressed to release the strap.

Two people are needed to remove a full-face crash helmet safely. One supports the head and neck, the other lifts the helmet. Move the helmet backwards and lift it until it is free of the chin. Then move the helmet forwards, so that it clears the base of the skull, and lift it straight off. If the helmet is removed, the head and neck must be supported until a surgical collar is fitted, otherwise serious injury could result.

Do not move an injured motorcyclist unless he or she is in immediate danger – there may be a neck injury.

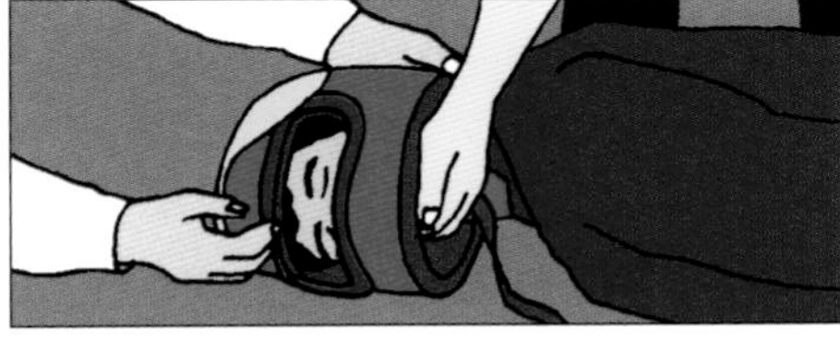

Safe removal of a motorcyclist's full-face helmet requires two people – one to support the head and neck, the other to lift the helmet – and careful use of the procedure described here.

First aid kits

By carrying a first aid kit you are better prepared to help yourself and others in the event of an accident. It may even save someone's life.

Your first aid kit should be clearly marked and easily accessible, and can be carried in any suitable plastic container, preferably a flexible and transparent one. Mark it 'First Aid'. Older first aid boxes carry a red cross on the lid but current legislation requires the cross to be green, and if you carry a home-made box it should be so marked. Any ointments or pain relievers must be only for your own use.

This box should contain sterile dressings in large, medium and small sizes, triangular bandages for use as slings or bandages, safety pins, plasters, scissors and a knife. You could carry anti-sting and scald ointments for minor mishaps which might impair your driving.

Today's tendency towards litigation makes it necessary to remember that you should not offer a casualty any kind of drugs, not even an aspirin or a paracetemol tablet, or stimulants such as coffee or alcohol, and you should not apply a self-adhesive plaster or ointment to a wound, burn or sting.

Fire

There is just one set of accident circumstances when you should break the rule and pull injured people from their vehicles. Although fire occurs in only a tiny proportion of accidents, it requires instant action and great presence of mind.

The fire may be caused by a short circuit from damaged wiring, in which case you should have plenty of time to deal with it as long as petrol is not seeping from a ruptured tank dangerously near it. If a crashed vehicle carries a fire extinguisher, aim it at the seat of the flames and keep up the discharge until the fire is out.

If the fire is in the engine bay, opening the bonnet can feed the fire with a draught of air, causing the flames to flare up. If you can, open the bonnet just enough to allow you to aim the fire extinguisher inside, but only if you can identify with certainty the source of the flames. If you cannot see where the fire is coming from before you open the bonnet a fraction, open it wide and be ready to act quickly if the fire expands – keep your head and hands low. If you can, break the electrical circuit feeding the fire by disconnecting the battery leads.

Many electronic devices on cars are encapsulated in fluorocarbon plastics. These are perfectly safe in normal use, but if subject to fire they can generate hydrofluoric acid residues that are exceedingly dangerous and toxic. You must not handle any encapsulated components that have been in a fire, either in an emergency or if salvaging parts – the only treatment is amputation.

A petrol fire is even more serious, calling for heroic action if anything is to be done to save people trapped inside the car. A petrol fire can often be avoided, however, by making sure there is no possibility of any sparks near the damaged car.

The car's ignition must always be switched off and no-one must smoke. No attempt should be made by anyone but the emergency services – normally the fire brigade – to cut away damaged metal to release occupants.

The fire brigade carry equipment for cutting injured people out of wrecked cars.

Accident procedures

Most accidents are minor collisions involving no injury to people, but even these should be treated seriously. The law demands that you give your name and address and insurance company details to the other driver and to anyone else, such as a police officer, who may reasonably require it. It is your responsibility to make sure you obtain these same details from the other driver. Remember to collect information from anyone else who saw the incident, but be quick about it because witnesses have a habit of melting away into the background.

Where severe damage is caused to vehicles it is best not to move them until the police have inspected the incident – but sometimes they cannot be moved anyway...

You are not required by law to inform the police if all these points are followed, but it is always advisable to do so if anyone is injured or there is an allegation of dangerous driving. Many people think that causing damage to a parked vehicle, perhaps by scraping the nose of your car along its wing, is part of the rough and tumble of life, but it is unethical – and illegal – to drive off without leaving a note of your name and address under the windscreen wiper. Would you like this done to you?

Where more severe damage is caused to vehicles, it is best not to move them until the police have inspected the incident and taken measurements. If you have a camera, photographs could be useful as evidence if the matter comes to court. Take your own measurements and make notes of exactly what happened so you can give precise information to your insurance company. The more detail you can provide, the better the chance, if the incident was someone else's fault, that his or her company and not yours will be paying up.

Take care not to say anything, either to the other driver or to the police, which you may later regret. It is always possible you may say things in the heat of the moment which may later be interpreted as acceptance of liability. Every insurer advises that you should leave assessment of blame to them.

Very minor collisions causing only superficial damage may result in a great deal of anger, but sometimes it is better to be philosophical if the incident is not your fault, and put the cost down to bad luck. On a busy road, other road users will not thank you for causing a traffic jam while you argue over a cracked tail light. The police also would not be pleased about being dragged into such an inconsequential matter which could never merit prosecution.

You may be fortunate in finding that the offending driver agrees to pay for your minor repairs but, if not, you are unlikely to be able to persuade the insurance company to pay. They would know that the cost, time and trouble of legal action would never be worthwhile to extract a small amount of money, and you would hardly want to go to your own insurer with a claim which would probably be exceeded by the cost of higher premiums in the future.

However annoying it may be at the time, you may have to put a minor knock down to experience.

If ever you see a 'hit and run' accident, try to write down as soon as possible the registration number, colour and make of the vehicle involved, a description of the incident and maybe even a description of the driver. Do not forget, though, that your first duty is always to the victim.

Motorway accidents

Do not 'rubber-neck' when you pass the scene of a motorway accident. The emergency services use this word for those ghoulish individuals who take their eyes off the road and look at the accident. Further accidents can, and do, occur when a driver is distracted from the job in hand.

Advanced checklist

- Absorb carefully the details contained in this chapter about accident procedure if you are one of the first on the scene. You must act swiftly and with great presence of mind.
- Carry a first aid kit and make sure you know how to use it.
- At minor accidents which involve no injury, your exchange of details with the other party should include names and addresses, vehicle details and names of insurance companies. Do not admit liability even if you feel you were at fault.

Driving abroad

Hints and tips

French *autoroute* police can calculate your average speed between toll booths and issue a ticket on this evidence alone.

Driving abroad always demands extra care but as an advanced driver you should be able to take it all in your stride. Here are a few pointers.

- Concentrate hard on the job in hand – not just at first (that comes automatically) but even after you have a few hundred kilometres under your belt.
- Most 'driving on the wrong side' incidents occur when you are relaxed, especially if you have parked on the opposite (left) side of the road and there is no other traffic about. Take special care when leaving filling stations, shops or laybys.
- If you think it will help, stick a 'Drive On The Right' message on the dashboard or steering wheel.
- Keep well back when planning an overtaking manoeuvre. In a right-hand drive car you will need extra distance to pull out and check the road ahead is clear.
- Do not rely on the advice of your front seat passenger when planning to overtake.
- A speeding offence is the most common reason for being stopped, so make sure you know the limits in each country you enter.
- Continental traffic laws by and large equate to ours, but they are often enforced with great firmness – and being a visiting tourist may not get you off the hook. For example, French *autoroute* police can impose on-the-spot fines for speeding, payable in cash, travellers' cheques or by major credit card. Can't pay? Then they may impound your car until you can. Remember they can calculate your average speed between toll booths and issue a ticket on this evidence alone.
- Keep to other rules too. 'Stop' signs mean just that, and if you roll across one you might just find a police officer waiting to step out and catch you.
- Watch out for continuing use of the 'priority to the right' rule in France. Unless there are signs or road markings to the contrary, drivers approaching from your right at junctions may emerge unexpectedly. Many French people have lived by this rule throughout their driving lives and sometimes still stick to it, although the French authorities have generally brought their practice into line with the rest of Europe. Particular care is needed in towns.
- Take a red warning triangle to set up down the road if a breakdown forces you to stop in a dangerous spot. Not all countries insist on it, but self-preservation alone justifies carrying one and using it.
- At traffic lights you will often encounter a continually flashing amber light. It means you should cross the junction with great caution and be prepared to give way.
- Keep a special eye out for cyclists, especially in Holland, Belgium and Denmark. Local custom, as well as the law, expects cyclists to be treated with courtesy and consideration – unlike the treatment they often get in Britain. Often they have right of way where one of the many cycle tracks crosses a road.
- Do not argue with trams! They usually have priority over other traffic and systems are expanding in many urban areas.
- Do not set yourself unmanageable daily mileages. Fatigue sets in easily on long motorway runs and drowsiness can be heightened by a big midday meal. Take it easy, enjoy yourself and let your passengers enjoy their journey too.
- Buy a good road atlas and plan your route properly. If you are in no rush, choose quiet roads.

Stay alert on quiet roads in wonderful scenery – 'driving on the wrong side' incidents tend to occur when there is no traffic to remind you.

Towing

Safety considerations

The IAM operates a special towing test in partnership with The Camping & Caravanning Club. (The latter's manoeuvring course is now an essential pre-requisite to the IAM's towing test). Because of the potential dangers of towing trailers, it is essential to follow basic safety rules.

Always ensure that the tyres on both your vehicle and your trailer or caravan are in good condition and correctly inflated. Not doing so could lead to a sudden blow-out and loss of steering and braking control. Always keep the nose weight on the trailer fairly high: a downward force of 25-75kg usually ensures stabiltiy.

Check that the tow-ball is fully latched home, that safety chains and emergency brake pulls are in position, and that all the lights on the trailer (which must carry your vehicle's registration number) are working.

Ensure that any load is properly secured and never allow passengers or pets to travel in a caravan or on a trailer. Last of all, release the parking brake and any overrun brake catch on the trailer's drawbar.

Manoeuvring

Reversing a car and trailer combination is always the hardest manoeuvre, especially for a novice. If you wish to make the trailer swing to the right, you must begin by reversing to the left to pivot the trailer onto the right line, and then alter your steering so that your vehicle starts to travel in the right direction too.

This is an art which requires a special technique and must be practised, preferably in a wide open space out of harm's way.

Visibility, speed and traffic

The 'getting away from it all factor' more than compensates for the extra difficulties involved in towing a caravan.

Always allow for the extra width of a trailer, particularly in built-up areas, when overtaking cyclists and parked vehicles. Remember that the trailer will cut in closer to the kerb than the car itself when negotiating junctions or sharp bends. It is essential to fit your car with mirrors that have extended arms to give yourself adequate rearward vision.

If your trailer or caravan is fairly stable, it is easy to let your speed build up to its 'normal' level without your noticing it. Generally you should be driving more slowly when towing, for reasons of legality, stability and braking. Find out about speed limits because they vary according to the design of trailer and type of road, and remember that you must not use the right-hand lane of a motorway when towing.

One of the biggest dangers on the open road is the dreaded swing. At certain speeds, many trailers and caravans can start oscillating from side to side, creating a pendulum effect which produces greater and greater swings. Slow down gently if this occurs: do not brake heavily as this could cause the trailer to swing more violently. Stop as soon as possible to adjust the weight on the trailer so that more force bears down on the drawbar.

When towing, avoid causing frustration to other drivers. You may have all the time in the world if you are on holiday with a caravan, but other people going about their daily business will want to make better progress. Pull into a layby for a minute or two whenever traffic builds up behind you. On a twisty road with few overtaking opportunities, it is thoughtful to pull in just to let a single car past. Be aware that many drivers have an antipathy to caravans simply because their owners seem unconcerned about the delays they cause.

Braking

The extra weight of a trailer or caravan means that braking distances are considerably increased. Safe towing requires you always to look a long way ahead and identify potential hazards at an early stage. Always leave yourself enough time to slow down smoothly.

Never forget that you are towing, stable as your trailer might be. Leaving insufficient room for braking is a classic mistake made by drivers with little experience of towing.

Advanced checklist

- If you use a trailer or caravan, take the towing test operated by the IAM.
- Allow for greater stopping distances when towing.
- You are bound by different legal requirements when towing: make sure you understand how the law applies to you.
- To avoid causing frustration to other drivers, pull over if traffic builds up behind.

7 THE ADVANCED DRIVING TEST

What the test involves

Why you should take the advanced test

Are you as good a driver as you think you are? The most experienced driver is one who never stops learning, for road conditions are continuously evolving and you need to practise your skills no matter how expert you may become – or think you have become.

The L-test is only an elementary examination. The real learning starts when you can throw away your L-plates and begin the acquisition of mature driving skills. Many people realise this, and there comes a time when they want to reassure themselves that their driving is developing along the right lines.

This is why the Institute of Advanced Motorists exists. It was founded in 1956 as a non-profit making organisation and is registered as a charity. It is dedicated to the promotion of road safety by encouraging motorists to take pride in good driving. By taking the Advanced Driving Test, you can measure the progress you have made since passing the basic test.

The IAM seeks to promote skill with responsibility. If every driver had the enthusiasm to pass the IAM test and the self-discipline to drive to a high standard all the time, there would be a dramatic fall in the casualties on British roads.

More than a quarter of a million people have taken the Advanced Driving Test, with a pass rate of about 70 per cent. Over 500 leading British companies have put their drivers through it, resulting in lower accident rates and reduced insurance costs.

Taking the Advanced Driving Test enables you to measure the progress you have made in your driving since passing the basic test.

Preparing for the test

The IAM has about 200 Groups around the country and overseas. Groups have schemes to advise prospective candidates on preparing for the test. The approaches vary from informal classroom sessions to on-the-road advice from skilled and experienced IAM members.

Some Group members hold a Police Advanced Driving Certificate, the highest driving qualification in Britain, so you can expect a high degree of expertise. If you like the idea of joining a club whose main interest is in advanced driving, contact with your local Group should be your first move.

Some professional driving instructors offer tuition to advanced level, but it is also possible for thoughtful drivers to pass the test without special instruction. Studying all the guidance in this book and applying it every time you drive should enable you to pass without too much difficulty.

You can apply to take the Advanced Driving Test by contacting the Institute of Advanced Motorists at the address on page 80.

The test format

Debriefing after the test: the examiner may have praise, and constructive criticism will be offered even if you have passed.

A test takes about 90 minutes and covers 35-40 miles. The route incorporates all kinds of road conditions, including motorways (if there is one within reach), dual-carriageways, congested urban areas, main roads, narrow country lanes and residential streets.

You are not expected to give a display of fancy driving: you should handle your car in the steady, workmanlike way you drive every day. The examiner does not, for example, expect exaggeratedly slow speeds or excessive signalling.

You are required to drive with due regard for road, traffic and weather conditions, observing all speed limits. You will need to show that you can drive briskly and that you are not afraid to cruise at the legal limit when circumstances permit–progress with safety. You will be asked to reverse around a corner, manoeuvre into a parking space and possibly make a hill start.

There are no trick questions and no attempts to catch you out. Throughout the test the examiner will give you route instructions, and there will be spot checks on your powers of observation. You are no longer required to give a running commentary during part of your test, but doing so can confirm the quality of your observation.

The examiner, who will always hold a Police Advanced Driving Certificate and have a traffic patrol background, will tell you whether you have passed or failed at the end of the test. There may be praise, and certainly constructive criticism will be offered even if your standard of driving is good enough to pass. The test is conducted in a spirit of friendliness, not intimidation.

Occasionally the examiner will identify a potentially dangerous fault, and may draw your attention to this during the test. A quiet word will help you to correct it. You will not be failed for minor faults, but infringements of the law cannot be condoned.

All examiners hold a Police Advanced Driving Certificate and have a traffic patrol background.

Who and where?

Anyone with a full UK or EC driving licence, including disabled drivers with suitably adapted cars, can take the test provided they have not been convicted of a serious traffic offence in the past three years. You can take the test in almost any car which you provide yourself, most vans and trucks, and certain three-wheelers.

You will not have to travel far because the IAM has a network of over 130 test routes nationwide. The examiner will fix a mutually acceptable date and time, and will meet you at a pre-arranged rendezvous.

You can take the test in almost any car which you provide yourself.

After the test

The duty to set an example

As a member of the Institute of Advanced Motorists, your conduct on the road will be an example to others.

Try to improve your technique and keep analysing your driving to make sure you are not slipping into bad habits.

You may consider repeating the Advanced Driving Test every few years in order to sharpen your skills.

Benefits of IAM membership

When you pass the Advanced Driving Test and become a member of the Institute of Advanced Motorists, a few of the many benefits available to you include:

- **Badge** The right to display the IAM's badge and certificate, providing visible proof of the high standards that you have achieved.
- **Insurance** An introduction to insurers who may give special terms – the discount can be as much as 20 per cent – subject to a satisfactory proposal.
- **Magazine** *Advanced Driving*, which is published every four months, is produced for IAM members and written by people who take a keen interest in driving.
- **Social activities** The chance to meet other men and women who share your outlook on driving. You can decide to join one of the IAM Groups and take part in the events and activities they organise.
- **Discounts** These are available from a wide range of organisations, including the AA.

Among the many discounts available are special rates with the AA.

Institute of Advanced Motorists
IAM House
510 Chiswick High Road
London W4 5RG
Tel: 020 8996 9600
Fax: 020 8996 9601
Website: www.iam.org.uk
E-mail: enquiries@iam.org.uk

11 Patricks Court
Patrick Street
Kilkenny
Republic of Ireland
Tel: 00 353 56 777 1778
Fax: 00 353 56 777 1779
Website: www.irishadvanced motorist.ie
E-mail: ireland@iamfleet.com